Bright Fields

A Memoir

Louise Knolle Pettigrove

For Mary Jane.
With love,
Louise

1/22/024

Cover Illustration:
Henry's Barn oil painting by John Pettigrove

Earth's crammed with heaven,

And every common bush afire with God.

Elizabeth Barrett Browning

For Pearson, A.W., Kathy, Carolyn, Charles, Janice, Ginny, Joe, Margaret, Tom, and Susan

And in memory of the thousands of gentle Jerseys who graced Knolle Jersey Farms

Contents

Figures

Preface

My cousin Kathy and my husband John were in the hospital room with me when Dr. Stanley Appel and his team of residents gave the ALS diagnosis. Dr. Appel told me that maybe I would live a long time with ALS, and the white-coated residents nodded in unison. They filed out as quickly as they had come in, and the room fell silent.

I wondered what John was thinking. He was a physician. Maybe he would have some answers. But John was slumped in his chair, looking at the floor. Kathy, who'd fallen off of a mountain while rock climbing the previous year, was perched on the windowsill. She broke the silence.

"Well, Weegee, you sure knocked me out of the saddle. All I have is a broken back."

We all laughed, and I could breathe again. After a while, I told Kathy I thought I could live ten more years. She reached toward me.

"Oh, Weegee, you might not."

She'd just read in the waiting room that people diagnosed with ALS only live 3 to 5 years, if they're lucky.

That was 19 years ago.

Years later, it was Kathy who died of ALS, and I've ended up writing this book. I'd always hoped Kathy would write the story we Knolle cousins had shared, the story about our childhood on the Farm. She'd gotten a PhD in literature and was an exceptional writer.

Because I have ALS, I've been forced to slow down and do the things that matter most. So I've written this book for my children and grandchildren and for my cousins and their children and grandchildren.

There were twelve of us Knolle cousins, all born within six years of each other. We grew up shaped by our grandparents, our wider family, and our shared experience of Knolle Jersey Farms in the 1950s.

What's difficult for me about writing a book based on our lives together is that I can only tell the stories from my perspective. All of us cousins remember things differently because we experienced them differently, and I regret if I have left out events that are important to them. Some of the dialogue I remember. It contains phrases or remarks that I remember people saying. I didn't take notes, so it's not exact. In other areas, I wrote dialogue based on my knowledge of the situation and on what people have told me about events. In every chapter, I tried to be accurate. There are stories and people that weren't included because I didn't have adequate knowledge to render them in an accurate faction.

And now, as I write this preface and look over *Bright Fields,* I feel gratitude for my life and the people in my life.

I couldn't have written *Bright Fields* without Pam Behrends-Gouverne, Phyllis Finley, Jan Hilton, and Cindy Sullivan—the "Jungsters"—who have kept me questioning. Or without Linda Savage, who's kept me moving, Mary Beth Davis, who's kept me writing, and Bill Mays who's given technical support.

Olga Marines has made my life easier.

Kaj Schimmel has been my advisor and my best spiritual friend.

Geordie Schimmel has shown me how to live courageously. For twenty years he's lived with multiple sclerosis while finishing law school, working full time, and raising four children with Amber, his wife.

And John Pettigrove has made my life good.

Part One: The Wade Ranch 1890s-1985

Introduction

Bright Fields begins with the story of my mother Mary Margaret Buchanan Knolle and the Wade Ranch.

Her family, the Buchanans, married into the John Wade family, who owned the 85,000-acre Wade Ranch near present-day Sandia. John Wade had immigrated from Yorkshire, England, in 1852, and in 1876, he'd purchased land on the Casa Blanca Land Grant just across the Nueces River from San Patricio. In 1894, Lou Ella Buchanan married John Wade's son Wallis, and they built the Big House and created the historic Wade Ranch.

My mother's father Floyd Buchanan was the youngest brother of Lou Ella Buchanan Wade. In 1931, Floyd moved his wife Louise Mason and his daughter Mary Margaret to the Ranch, so he could work for Lou Ella. At the Wade Ranch, Floyd encountered a situation that tore his young family apart.

Mary Margaret left the Wade Ranch firmly behind her when she married Ed Knolle at age 16. Louise Mason left the Ranch as well. The problems Floyd endured while there ruined his health, and he died at age 46.

As a child growing up near the Wade Ranch, I sensed a mysterious darkness surrounding that big white house on the hill. I also noticed whenever I would enter a room, talk of the Wade Ranch would stop. I began to understand that my grandmother's pain was linked to Lou Ella Buchanan Wade.

Over the next four decades, I pieced together a story that is sad and wide-sweeping.

In Part One of *Bright Fields*, I've interwoven the lives of my Buchanan family and the Wade Ranch. I've chosen to narrate different parts of this tale as I encountered them to show my own growth in awareness.

Fig. 1 The Big House, Wade Ranch, Sandia, Texas, circa 1930s

Going, Going, Gone … (1985)

I'd arrived late to the Wade Ranch auction. Folding chairs had been placed on the lawn, and the auctioneer stood above the crowd. I found a seat, took a breath, and looked around. I recognized only a few people and felt like I had no business being there.

I was 43 years old, and I'd come to the auction to see where my mother Mary Margaret Buchanan had spent so many painful years growing up. Although my own house was only a few miles down the road, this was my first visit to the Wade Ranch. Mama had never returned to the Ranch after the funeral of her father Floyd. The funeral had been held in the front parlor of the Big House, but Mama and her mother hadn't been allowed to sit with the family. Lou Ella had insisted that Floyd's widow and daughter sit in a room nearby. Now Lou Ella was gone. They were selling all her stuff, and I was there to see the end of it all.

"Here it is folks—your chance to purchase this antique corset worn by Lou Ella herself."

The auctioneer stood on one of the side porches of the Big House. He held the corset up high with both hands and then lowered it and began to hum and move as if dancing with it, all the while wiggling and dipping the corset. The crowd burst into laughter, and I cringed to see my family's privacy exposed in such a way. I realized that Lou Ella would have been way too slender to wear that corset. It had probably belonged to my great-grandmother, Margaret Pinkie Buchanan.

Fig. 2 Margaret Pinkie Buchanan, 80 yrs.
in front of the original Wade Ranch house, her home for
many years, May 1937

Pinkie had been a loving and gentle soul, but no one in that crowd even knew she'd existed. No one in the crowd knew that on that very porch, Pinkie had taught little Mary Margaret Civil War songs. No one knew the story about the Yankee soldiers, who'd camped right below Pinkie's family plantation in Tennessee. Pinkie had been five then, and she'd sneaked away from her family and gone down the front road to see the Yankees. One of the soldiers had told her about his little girl, who looked just like Pinkie. When Pinkie'd returned to her family, no one would speak to her because she'd sat on the lap of a Yankee. Pinkie also told Mary Margaret the story about the Yankees leaving the plantation and taking her elderly father's thoroughbred horses. He'd cried out, "My darlings, they're taking my darlings."

That porch where Pinkie had told stories to Mama circled three sides of the Big House. The Big House had been the operating center of the historic Wade Ranch for six decades. Lou Ella Buchanan had married Wallis Wade in 1894, and right after, they'd designed and built the two-story house. It had big columns and was painted white with dark green shutters.

Behind the Big House was the original ranch house where Mama had lived with her parents and her grandmother, Pinkie. The land had been purchased by John Wade in the 1870s. and Mama had spent much of her young life riding her paint pony across its thousands of acres.

I hadn't been there long when the auctioneers took a lunch break. My cousin, Tommy Priestly, made his way over to greet me and thank me for coming. Tommy was a few years older than I, and we'd met from time to time over the years in Corpus. His wife Karen greeted me as well. Their kindness told me they knew how hard it was for me to be there.

Tommy asked if there was anything I wanted from

the Big House, and I told him about the only thing that Mama had asked me to get. She wanted the framed copy of "The Lord's Prayer" written in calligraphy that had hung in her bedroom when she was a child. Tommy and I spotted "The Lord's Prayer" on a table. As soon as I saw it, I winced at its sentimentality. I couldn't see how anyone, even Mama, would want it.

Mama could've asked me to find more important things. A soldier's trunk with a WWI uniform and gas mask had been advertised. She'd told me that it had to have been her father's. He'd been the only one of the four Buchanan brothers who'd fought in France. But the uniform and gas mask were gone. They must've been stolen or taken by family much in the same way I was now getting "The Lord's Prayer."

After lunch, the crowd reconvened. Before I could get to my seat, the auctioneer held up a large painting of a sweet-looking woman in pink, looking down at a bouquet of flowers. He told the crowd it was a portrait of Lou Ella Wade. I found out later that the portrait was more likely that of Mollie Madray, Wallis's first wife, who'd died a short time after they'd married. That's also when Mama told me that after Lou Ella's baby died at birth, she'd almost never worn anything but black, certainly not pink. And Lou Ella probably wouldn't have looked down at a bouquet. In the pictures I've seen of her, she'd always held her chin high, and her eyes seemed to pierce the camera.

All my life I'd heard stories of Lou Ella and how she'd hurt people close to me. I'd learned early that Lou Ella was impatient and cold toward Mama. She'd been cruelest to Mama's mother, and I'd seen my grandmother's eyes become hard and empty over the years. I'd known that she'd failed to keep her promises to Mama's father. My grandfather had become so financially dependent on Lou Ella that he was unable to provide for his own family or keep them together.

I'd only seen Lou Ella one time. It was 1947, and I was five. I was in Lichtenstein's Department Store with Mama and my brother Charles. Mama had dressed us up for the shopping trip. Charles was three. He always attracted attention because he was so handsome. I had on a starched pink dress and a white pinafore. Mama would say, "Pretty is as pretty does," so I was on my best behavior.

Mama, Charles, and I were in the elevator on our way to the children's department on the fourth floor. On the second floor the door opened, and two old ladies got in. One of them was dressed all in black. She stared straight ahead and didn't look at us. The other lady peeked at me and then looked down at her feet. Mama stood straight and quiet. She squeezed my hand so tight it hurt. I thought the ladies were mean to upset Mama, and I squinted my eyes at them. At the fourth floor, we all got out and went different ways. Mama told me they were her aunts, Lou Ella and Arminta. She said they never talked to her anymore.

Lou Ella may have had second thoughts about that incident. Years later when I was in high school in Mathis, I heard she'd tell people I looked like her.

❖

The auction finally ended. As I walked toward my car, my cousin, Pearson Knolle, came up to me. "Louise, Tommy told me to make sure you get this."

He handed me a framed panel of three photographs. The photographs were of my grandfather Floyd in his formal dress uniform as a cadet at West Texas Military Academy in San Antonio. The backing of the wooden frame was a poster of a young girl holding a pack of Old Mill Cigarettes. Over that advertisement in large block letters, Lou Ella had printed:

At my death or before,
this picture of Floyd Buchanan
is to go to his granddaughter,
Louise Knolle Schimmel.

Lou Ella Wade

I was stunned by this gesture. I wanted to feel grateful, but it was too little too late.

Mollie's Letters (1891-1892)

I'm thinking about Mollie Madray and Wallis Wade when I realize I've pulled off the road to get a better look at the Nueces River.

It's still the same muddy river with the same steep banks that I knew as a child. Those were happy days with my cousins, learning to swim, catching minnows. We saw the river as a barrier and tried to make a bridge of sand so we could get to the other side.

The River Bridge linking Sandia and Mathis is a concrete structure built in the 1930s. The Nueces River still flows beneath, but you'd have to know it's there, or you wouldn't see it. For me as a child, the River Bridge was a gateway between my home on our farm and the outside world of my Methodist Sunday School, my elementary school, and my best friends, Erin, Mary Wayne, Patsy, Eileen, Carol Ann and Jeanette.

But now for me as an adult, I'm just making another trip to the Farm. I'm in partnership with my father Ed and we're making a change from dairying to running beef cattle, so there's a lot to do. I handle the office part of things, bookkeeping, payroll, getting bills paid. Ed still likes to work with the cattle. I don't think he'll ever quit. Geordie, Kaj, and I have lived in Corpus since the divorce. We've found a good school and church there and made new friends.

As I look toward the river, it occurs to me that this spot on the Nueces had often created a barrier for Mollie Madray and Wallis Wade when they'd been courting so long ago. When they met at the Methodist church in Mathis, they'd lived on opposite sides of the river. She lived in Mathis, and he lived on the Wade Ranch. No bridge had existed then, and when the Nueces flooded, Wallis couldn't have crossed it to see the girl he'd decided to marry. Wallis had been 26 and was already a respected rancher. He would soon inherit the bulk of the Wade Ranch from his father, John Wade.

Though I wasn't directly related to Wallis, I'd heard many stories about him and the Wade Ranch from my mother Mary Margaret. She'd lived there as a child with her parents, Floyd and Louise Buchanan, and her grandmother, Pinkie Buchanan.

Fig. 3 Nueces River Bridge, circa 1916

I'd first heard the story of John Wade when I'd taken my mother to see the Wade Ranch shortly after I'd gone to the auction of the contents of the house. Mama had left the Ranch at 15 and only returned once at 20 for the funeral of her father. The day I'd taken her back was the first time she'd been there in 43 years.

Mama and I had arranged for her cousin, Tommy Priestly, to meet us at the Wade Ranch. He waved to us from the porch as our car approached the Big House and greeted us as we walked up the porch steps.

"Come on in. Good to see you, Mary Margaret. It's been a while..." He gave her a hug and reached his hand out to me.

The rooms in the house were almost empty of furnishings, but Tommy led us down a long hall.

"You'd probably like to see the house in the back first, Mary Margaret. I know that's where you used to live. A few years ago, they built this hall connecting the two houses. It makes a good place for Lantie's books."

I'd forgotten that Lou Ella's nieces and nephews, even Mama, called her "Lantie." Mama showed me her bedroom, and we looked around the little house we moved into the kitchen, Tommy pointed to a hole in the wall.

"That's the hole from the bullet that hit John Wade."

And then he and Mama told me the story. The hole was made in 1895 by a bullet after it passed through John Wade's body. One evening, John Wade and his family had heard a knock at the door, and he'd picked up a kerosene lamp and gone to see who was there. He was immediately shot in the stomach. The commotion caused by the rest of the family in an adjacent room must have frightened the would-be assassin away.

They say that John Wade had been attacked by a man hired by a disgruntled heir to the Wade Ranch. After the shooting, the Wades moved into the hotel a few miles away in Wade City because they were afraid to stay on the Ranch ever again. John Wade had lived only three more years. He bled to death from the old bullet wound when he bent over and tore some adhesions.

John Wade had immigrated as a young man to Texas from Yorkshire, England, in 1852. During the next two decades, he became a sheep rancher in the Nueces Valley and began buying land on the old Casa Blanca Land Grant. He founded the Wade Ranch sometime in the 1870's.

In the 1880's, he established Wade City nearby with a church, a hotel, a lumberyard, and 150 inhabitants. After John Wade died in 1898, Wallis, his second oldest son, inherited over 20,000 acres of the Wade Ranch. Wallis had already buried one wife, Mollie Madray, and then had married Lou Ella Buchanan.

Nowadays, no one remembers anything about Wallis' first wife, Mollie Madray, except Mama. As a child, she'd spent a lot of time with her Uncle Wallis and seen a large portrait of Mollie. The portrait had hung in the Big House which Wallis and Lou Ella had designed and built in 1894.

After Tommy had shown us the bullet hole, Mama and I went back through the long hallway into the Big House. She'd pointed to a spot above the staircase. "That's where Lou Ella hung the big portraits, one of herself and one of Mollie. Mollie was wearing a long pink dress, and Lou Ella was in black."

Now, three years after that visit to the Wade Ranch, I know more about Mollie and more about the barriers that can separate a young couple. Mollie and Wallis wrote to each other while they were courting. Mollie's letters must have been saved by Wallis and then by Lou Ella. I'd found the letters in a satin envelope along with some old family photographs which had been given to me for safekeeping.

Mollie's fifteen letters tell the story of the growing

intimacy between her and Wallis. They reveal a self-confident and attractive young woman who was reluctant to enter into a shallow relationship. She'd already experienced one broken engagement and didn't want another.

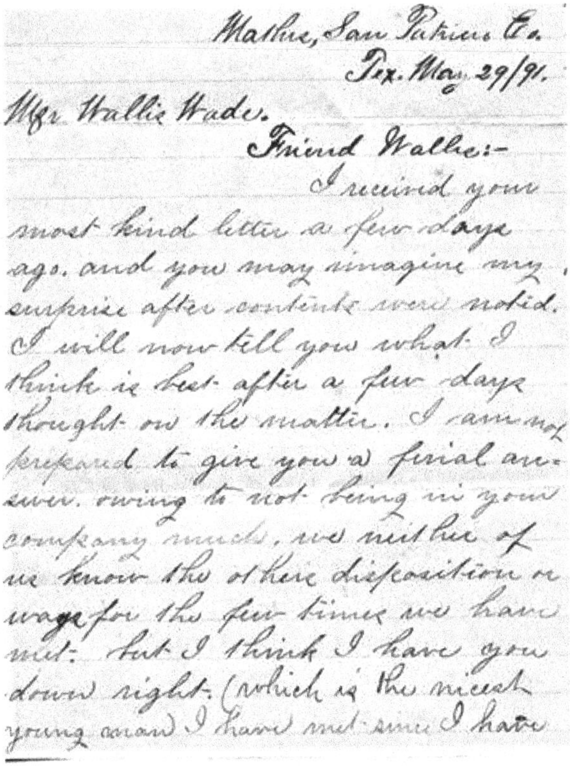
Mathis, San Patricio Co.
Tex. May 29/91.
Mr. Wallis Wade.
Friend Wallis:-
I received your most kind letter a few days ago. and you may imagine my surprise after contents were noted. I will now tell you what I think is best after a few days thought on the matter. I am not prepared to give you a final answer. owing to not being in your company much, we neither of us know the others disposition or ways for the few times we have met: but I think I have you down right (which is the nicest young man I have met since I have

Fig. 4 Mollie's first letter to Wallis
May 29, 1891, page 1

In 1891 Mollie was two years younger than Wallis and lived in Mathis with her family. At one of the dances, she'd gone to, she'd been voted "most popular girl" in Mathis. In May of that year, she received a letter from Wallis indicating his desire to marry her. She wrote back, "I propose waiting for several months, giving each time to know more about the other before entering into an engagement." They began to see each other frequently, usually at church, and they would correspond until the next Sunday or until they managed to meet again.

One of the barriers Wallis and Mollie encountered in their relationship was the Nueces River between them. It often flooded, and crossing it would've been impossible on horseback or with a horse and buggy. A ferry had been there since 1877, but it didn't run in bad weather. In September 1891, Mollie wrote, "So [I] guess you have had plenty of rain. We heard the river was up until today, so Joe and I would not start over to see you all: seems as if fate were against me getting over there."

After six months, Wallis was beginning to grow tired of the difficulties in seeing her, and he saw her apparent hesitation as another barrier. When he stopped answering her letters, Mollie began to worry about losing him. She sent a letter, saying:

> I've concluded to write and ask if you have forgotten my existence. Thought probably some other girl is ahead of me. And should [I] not wonder if there was? There being so many more attractive than poor little me. I do not wonder at your withdrawing your affections for you have certainly been sufficiently tried.

Their correspondence resumed. Mollie began to understand she was in love with Wallis when, at the conclusion of an argument between them, she'd noticed he was crying. "I did not realize how it would hurt you until you cried. I felt I knew you better than ever before." When Mollie realized how much she cared for him, she began to write more openly. On Christmas Eve, Mollie wrote, "I feel somehow as if you had found another girl. It ought not to make any difference with me, but I really do feel jealous. I sometimes think I care for you more than I thought I did."

In January of 1892, Mollie had finally made up her mind to marry Wallis. She wrote, "If you have not forgotten what I promised the evening we went riding, come tomorrow week 'on Sunday', and I will tell you something, unless you have learned to care for some other girl, then of course I can't."

By February 9th, Mollie had given Wallis her answer, and she wrote to assure him:

> "Now Wallis, I have given you my promise, and don't you think for a moment I will break it...You spoke of having the marriage earlier than June! I can't promise to yet but may consent for it to be the latter part of April. . . .
> I have not yet mentioned anything to Mama or Papa or anyone. Will soon tell Mama."

Mollie's letters also tell of visits to friends and family, visits which often stretched into weeks. And now that Mollie was engaged, she became the object of teasing. "I think I will go home Tuesday or Wednesday. I have been having a very good time here ... They tried to tease me a little about you but were not at all successful."

In a letter written in March, Mollie explained about some comments from friends and relatives who had tried to influence her:

> Wallis, you do not blame me for answering you the way I did! Did you? I just tell you I did not know you enough to know my own mind, and I had a good deal to work against too: you have been told things on me and so have I on you. But I would not believe until I found out for myself. As to your talking, I have found out that the more I know you, the more you talk, true, you do not talk as much as most young

men; but I am not afraid of your not talking enough. What you don't talk, I will make up for you.

Molly wasn't swayed by the gossip, and by March 19, she was counting the days until their marriage. "The time isn't two months off now last Friday." But the biggest barrier of all, Mollie's health, soon became the couple's overriding concern. Her first mention of measles occurs in late March. "I guess next Sunday I will have the measles, for Davis has broken out with them today." She'd been right and soon was sick herself.

Mollie was optimistic about her recovery even when she was very ill. On April 19th, she wrote, "This is the first day I have sat up in 5 days. If it were not for the fevers, I think I would have been well by now." In the April 19th letter, she tells him, "I am so weak, more so than when I was sick with fever last summer. I guess you begin to think what you heard about me being an invalid is about so. Sure has been that way for the last three weeks."

The last letter from Mollie was written on April 26, 1892. She was getting ready to go back to the doctor and was expecting a quick and full recovery. It seems though that Wallis was quite worried. He'd asked Mollie if she believed in prayer, and she'd answered, "Indeed I do. Would be a poor Methodist if I did not and was taught from a child to kneel down and say my prayers every night." It seems that Mollie and Wallis did marry late in May at her parents' home in Mathis.

There's another letter that was saved in the packet with Mollie's letters. It's from Mollie's mother. She's writing after the wedding and expressing worry and concern:

Dear daughter,
I am sorry that you are having fevers again. Be

sure and tell Dr how you have been and felt all along since you had the measles. If I come, I will be at the train. You and Wallis come Saturday if the river is low enough.

Mollie's poor health continued, and she died only months after the wedding. Wallis buried her in the Wade Cemetery on the Ranch where he would later be placed next to her. His second wife, Lou Ella, would be buried on his other side. Mollie's tombstone says simply:

Mollie Madray Wade
1868-1892

Today, that tombstone, half-covered by cactus, and the 15 love letters written in a clear flourishing hand are all I know that's left of Mollie Madray.

Fig. 5 Mollie Madray's gravestone
Wade Cemetery, Jim Wells Co., Texas

I notice my watch. I need to get on to the Farm. The lines from Psalm 103 come to me.

> As for mortals, their days are like grass: they
> flourish like a flower of the field.
> The wind passes over it, and it is gone...

Fig. 6 Aerial view of the Big House, circa 1930s

Into the Web (1930-1943)

I'm not sure if you or anyone else around here knows my grandmother's side of the story. I'm 70, and I've been hearing parts of it all my life. People say that my great-aunt Lou Ella Buchanan Wade destroyed my grandmother's life, and I want you to know the story as I've heard it, the story of what happened to my Nana.

Even when I was 12, my cousins and I had already known that Lou Ella was somehow dangerous.

"Faster, drive faster—the witch might get us."

We were squealing at my aunt Dorothy who was driving us over the River Bridge on our way to school in Mathis. We'd just gotten a clear view of the Big House on top of a far-away hill. My great-aunt Lou Ella Wade lived there.

By the time I'd gotten to fifth grade, I'd heard

many stories about Lou Ella. My mother Mary Margaret Buchanan and my grandparents Floyd and Louise Mason Buchanan had lived on the Wade Ranch where Lou Ella was the dominating force. I knew she'd been hostile to Mama, but it was my cousins who'd imagined Lou Ella as an evil witch.

Later, when I was in my 30's, Mama had told me more stories about Lou Ella, and we'd spent many hours looking at old photographs from the Wade Ranch. I learned that the Big House was Lou Ella's creation. Right after she married Wallis Wade when she was 18, she envisioned and supervised construction of the house. When Wallis inherited the working ranch, she'd established the Big House as the Wade Ranch headquarters, and as Wallis' health declined, Lou Ella had directed ranch hands, oilmen, cattlemen, and lawyers, all from the screened-in veranda that ran across the back of the Big House.

Fig. 7 The Red Barn, circa 1930
Floyd Buchanan, 3rd from left; Wallis Wade, 4th from left

Mama had described how Lou Ella filled the room

with green plants, long before it had been popular to have them indoors. The veranda must have been flooded with soft light filtering through the screens and creating a welcoming contrast to the hot sun. Right outside the veranda, Lou Ella had placed outbuildings of importance to her. She included a little wooden house for storing her old magazines and put the chicken yard under a spreading mulberry tree. Her rose garden and a circular plant conservatory were nearby. The barn was painted red.

Fig. 8 Music Room, deerskin rug at lower left, circa 1930

Inside the Big House, Lou Ella had taken similar care with the furnishings. She'd decorated the house in the Victorian style of the time, and some old photographs show mantles with ornate mirrors, velvet settees, and a Roman chair. Framed family pictures were placed on every flat surface, and Mama told me that the phrase, "a place for everything and everything in its place," was etched into the 10-foot walls of the kitchen.

The music room had featured a grand piano positioned in front of a bay window. The window was hung with heavy, velvet curtains that looked like something Scarlett O'Hara might've worn. The Big House though was in Texas not the South. A large deerskin rug—with head and antlers intact was stretched out on the floor in front of the grand piano. The whitetail buck, ten-points, was shot by my grandfather, Floyd Buchanan.

Having the best quality for herself and for the house must have been important to Lou Ella. She'd had her stylish Victorian dresses and lace underclothing made in San Antonio, and she'd had household furnishings shipped from as far away as St. Louis. She had created a formal dining room for the many family members, friends, and business acquaintances who were always visiting. Mama told me that one time when she was 12, there was a special occasion. The adults had gathered for dinner in the dining room. Mama had been politely eating with the grown-ups and had had time to look around. Suddenly, she pointed to a picture of a waterfall, hanging on the opposite wall, and she announced, "That picture's upside down." And it was. It must've been upside down for years. Lou Ella's face turned red, and the guests tried to remain straight-faced. Mama told me she'd spent the rest of the day in her hide-a-way in the big mulberry tree with *Grimm's Fairy Tales*.

Now at age 70, I've heard even more stories about Lou Ella and found more of the old Wade Ranch letters and photographs, many of my grandparents, Floyd and Nana. I've realized how complicated the entire story is.

My great-aunt Lou Ella had been the oldest of nine surviving children of Pinkie and Sanford Buchanan, and my grandfather, Floyd, had been the youngest. Pinkie and Sanford were second cousins and had been raised on nearby plantations in Tennessee during the Civil War. After the war, they packed up and took their baby, Lou Ella, to Texas. The growing family slowly migrated westward from Corsicana in East Texas over to Weatherford, west of Ft. Worth. They continued farther west to Midway, now Midland. They eventually made their way by covered wagon to La Fruta on the Nueces River in South Texas. Their last child, Floyd, was born on the Wade Ranch.

For Lou Ella, life must have been hard. She was only one year old when her family left Tennessee. For the next 16 years, her father moved the family to find work, and her mother gave birth to nine more children.

As the oldest, Lou Ella must have helped her mother with the cooking and must have taken care of the children as they were born. She must have helped her father in the fields. She probably became strong, tough, and persuasive. And she must have longed for a permanent home with the stability and respect that would come with one. Perhaps, in a desire to get what she'd wanted, Lou Ella had learned to use people to her advantage

Her father got work for a while on the Wade Ranch, helping John Wade put in a large watermelon crop. John Wade's son Wallis was recently widowed and stood to inherit the Wade Ranch. Lou Ella met and married Wallis Wade. She was 18, and Wallis was 28.

Fig. 10 Lou Ella, 18, and Wallis Wade, 28, 1894

Fig. 9 The Sanford Buchanan Family, 1905
Front row, l. to r., Simmons, Floyd, Sanford holding
Lou Ella Rountree , Pinkie holding Roy Page, Gordon
Back row, Ezella, Arminta, Myrtle, Lou Ella, Della

A year after they married, Wallis and Lou Ella's baby boy died in childbirth, and within a year, her mother Pinkie gave birth to her last child, James Floyd. He would become my grandfather. Lou Ella loved Floyd deeply, and she and Wallis raised him as their own son. They sent him to West Texas Military Academy in San Antonio (later named Texas Military Institute), which must have been a sacrifice for them as ranchers in the early 1900s. In the spring of 1917, Floyd was a cadet at West Texas Military Academy and left to enlist in the Army to serve in World War I.

Fig. 11 Floyd Buchanan, 18 yrs.

But before he left for France in 1918, Floyd had fallen love with the beautiful and modest, intelligent and popular Louise Mason. Many years later, Nana confided to me that she'd overheard some girls talking during her senior year at San Antonio High School. "It's too bad Louise Mason can't afford any pretty clothes to wear. She's so beautiful."

Fig. 12 Louise Mason, 20 yrs., circa 1917

Louise came from a distinguished family of war

heroes, statesmen, and wealthy merchants going all the way back to the American Revolution. But by the time the Masons immigrated to Texas from Kentucky, they had little money and no position. Louise's mother ended up raising her eight children alone, and after the death of her oldest son's wife, she raised six more.

Floyd Buchanan and Louise Mason married on March 29, 1920, after he came home from France. Louise would become my grandmother, "Nana." My mother Mary Margaret was born the next year. For the next 10 years or so, Floyd and Louise Mason lived an independent life working and living in North Texas.

Fig. 13 Mary Margaret, 5 yrs., on the way to the drugstore to get ice cream, Hearne, Texas, 1926

Around 1930, Lou Ella began pressuring Floyd to return to the Wade Ranch and work for her. Floyd must have always felt strong ties to Lou Ella and Wallis and the place where he was born and raised, and he might have felt obligated to them. Louise explained what had happened. Wallis "was in very poor health at that time and Lou Ella said she needed Floyd to help her manage her affairs." She made many financial promises for their future. She convinced Floyd he would inherit the Ranch if he came to help her.

So, Floyd, Louise, and nine-year-old Mary Margaret moved into the old Wade farmhouse behind the Big House. They had to share the space with Floyd's widowed mother Pinkie. Lou Ella bought all their clothes, including clothes for my mother. My grandparents never received a salary. Nana did all the cooking for the Big House and the ranch hands. She handled the bookkeeping and record keeping for Lou Ella. At that time, Lou Ella was compiling her family's genealogy, and Nana did all the typing. My mother was an only child. She must have resented that her mother was so busy, and she wrote her first poem.

Rat-a-Tat-Tat
by Mary Margaret Buchanan, 1931

Rat-a-tat-tat the tipewriter goes
Over and o'r, over and o'r.
Hunting our ancestors high and low,
In every nook and corner go.

Rat-a-tat-tat and scratch away.
Day after night, night after day.

Feeby Tidus, Margaret, John,

All Buchanans in a line.
Some from Scotland, some from Ireland,
some from Englande too.
And for wills, there's a Hullabaloo.

Rat-a tat-tat the tipewriter goes
Over and o'r, over and o'r

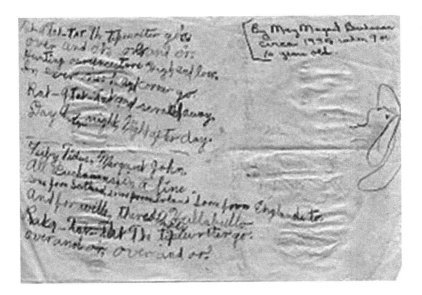

Fig. 14 Mary Margaret's poem written on scrap paper, 1931

Soon after my grandparents moved to the Ranch, Lou Ella became hostile to Nana, and as the years went on, Lou Ella openly turned against her. Nana explained that Lou Ella's, "own sisters have told me in years gone by that it was nothing but jealousy on her part because she could not stand for Floyd to put us before her. . . She made life unbearable for us from the beginning, but we stayed on to help her."

Lou Ella's jealousy had shaped Wallis' life as well. She'd become a dominant force in her family during all the years of moving, and she was used to being in charge. After she married Wallis, she began to dominate him. Wallis was 10 years older than Lou Ella and was often in poor health. Lou Ella kept a constant watchful eye on him. She wanted Wallis to stay close to the Big House. She even tried to isolate him from his own sister, Maggie McNeill, who lived on a nearby ranch. But Wallis managed to find ways to escape from Lou Ella's jealousy and keep some secrets from her.

Lou Ella never knew that Wallis often rode horseback to visit his sister, Maggie. He would ride through the back pastures with Mama, who was just 12 at the time. Wallis would manage to get word to his sister that they were coming, and they would arrive to find her waiting on the porch with a plate of cookies. Maggie was Wallis's closest sister, and they'd tell Mama stories about the job they'd had of skinning dead cows when they were 10 or 12. I'd learned about Lou Ella's desire to keep Wallis away from his family because Mama wrote about her memories, "Wallis Wade, my uncle by marriage, was one of the dearest, sweetest men I ever knew. He . . . suffered from Lou Ella's fierce jealousy because she resented his family."

Life on the Wade Ranch under Lou Ella's jealous eye finally became unbearable. Nana and Mama moved off the Ranch as soon as they were able. After years of going back and forth to San Antonio, Nana left to live there permanently. She stayed with relatives and began work as a practical nurse to support herself. Mama moved to Corpus to finish high school and live with her Aunt Ezella Buchanan Priestly. Taking matters into her own hands at the age of 16, she secretly married Ed Knolle. After she graduated from Corpus Christi High School, they settled into living on Knolle Jersey Farms, just a few miles from the Wade Ranch. Floyd remained on the ranch.

My grandfather Floyd would never escape Lou Ella and would never escape the Big House. Floyd managed the Ranch operations through the Great Depression and through the heat, drought, and floods of South Texas in the 1930s. Two oil fields were discovered, the Old Sandia Field and the Lou Ella Field. Hopes were high, but they came to nothing.

From the material I've seen of the Wade Ranch, I've come to understand the strength of Floyd Buchanan's character. The years at the Ranch must have been hard for him because of Lou Ella's hostility toward his wife and child. Floyd had many close friends in the area who understood the situation and tried to help him find employment and get away from Lou Ella. One of the close friends was Walter Foster of Corpus Christi, who wrote of Floyd as "my beloved friend." Mr. Foster understood Floyd's situation, and he found Floyd a good job with Armour Packing Company. But Lou Ella persuaded Floyd to stay and help her as she'd done every time he'd found employment off the Ranch.

Nana later described the trap my grandfather was in, "After the time I left the Ranch, Mrs. Wade watched every move he made, even going so far as to check the mileage and gasoline on his car." By August 1938, Floyd was desperate after trying to get away again. He wrote to Lou Ella and Wallis from a hotel in Alice, Texas:

> Dear Sister and Wallis,
> I don't know what to say but I want to say something and ask you to help me if you possibly can. I have been here for over a week and am trying to go to work here for a real estate company, but I am sick and don't know when I can. Could you send me $25.00? I need it, and if you can't I don't know what I will do. Besides that, I want you both to tell me that I

can write to you. God knows I love you both
and I always will. Please write me, if only a line,
as soon as you get this.
As ever
Floyd
% General Delivery, Alice, Texas

It seemed that my grandfather had no choice but to always return to the Ranch and to Lou Ella's jealousy. Two years later, in 1940, he wrote to my Nana, suggesting that Lou Ella had tried to interfere with his letter writing:

My dearest and only one,
I have been trying to write to you every day
since you were here but have not had the
proper chance where I could be at ease.
Sweetheart I was so glad to see you and God
only knows how I feel and how my heart ached
for you and worried about you—and I hope
and live for one thing and that is to have you
again like I want you but different somewhat
from the past.

In closing the letter, my grandfather assured her that he lived only for her, and he warned her that Lou Ella kept a close eye on his mail:

Please try to be happy until I see you,
Sweetheart—I love you Darling so much. God
knows I live only for you, and I feel like you
can't live or get along and be happy without
me looking after you. If you write send it to
Mary Margaret, Honey, 'cause she [Lou Ella]
gets the mail quite often. I love you,
Sweetheart.
Always,
Floyd

My grandfather Floyd Buchanan died unexpectedly in 1942 at the age of 46. He was buried with full military honors for his service in World War I. During his funeral at the Big House, Lou Ella had made Nana and Mama sit apart from the rest of the family in a separate room.

Lou Ella had even attempted to take the American flag presented to Nana as the widow. That carefully folded American flag came to be Nana's most precious possession. She kept it her entire life and planned to pass it on to my brother Charles because he was the only boy in our family. But Nana died before she gave it to anyone, and the flag disintegrated after 30 years in a garage closet.

I know now that Lou Ella had lured my grandfather Floyd and Nana to the Wade Ranch with very specific promises, promises she'd never kept. She'd never built the house she'd promised them. When she died in 1972, she'd not named Nana or Mama in her will nor left them the financial recompense she'd promised Floyd they would have after her death. Lou Ella's will included everyone in the Buchanan family, except for Mama.

With all her promises, Lou Ella had successfully manipulated Floyd, used Nana, and scarred Mama.

But it was my Nana's life that had been destroyed. Her married life became one of servitude to Lou Ella, her husband became dependent on Lou Ella's wishes, and her daughter grew up with hostility. At her own husband's funeral, Nana was humiliated and had to fight to be recognized as Floyd's wife. She did receive her monthly widow's pension of $35.00, but for fear of losing it, she never sought official employment. She moved from place to place, never staying too long at any one home. Her face became closed and pinched, her eyes vacant. She rarely smiled.

I want to remember Nana differently. I want to

remember Nana as the vivacious beauty who was often told she looked like Loretta Young. Nana was the one everyone at the Farm would call when someone was sick. When I was around eight, my uncle, Bob, told me what a great nurse she was, "You know, Weegee, your Nana saved your cousin's life. Ginny was a baby and had gotten very sick, and she came to our house and stayed night and day, nursing Ginny."

Fig 15A "Nana" Louise Mason Buchanan
Cleaning kitchen window! circa 1940s

Nana loved making little bouquets of wildflowers, and she would make me my favorite food, carrot salad. I can still see Nana twirling and dancing, singing, "When Grandma danced the minuet long ago, long ago ."

Fig 15 Louise Mason Buchanon, 45 yrs., Hot Springs, Ark.
On a trip with a patient to take the waters, 1943

The Lady and the Doctor (1925-1926)

The old roll-top desk stays in my mind. It's too heavy and too clumsy to be of practical use, yet it was a valued possession of my father Ed Knolle. The desk had originally belonged to Dr. J.W. Williams, the only doctor in Sandia for many years. Dr. Williams had delivered my father into the world in 1912.

I am linked to Dr. Williams through my great-aunt, Lou Ella Buchanan Wade. Lou Ella's brother, Tom Buchanan, had married Dr. Williams' daughter Adeline. Adeline and Tom were newly married in 1919 when Tom died of typhoid fever caught from cleaning out a cistern at the Wade Ranch.

Fig. 16 Dr. J. W. Williams, circa 1920s

What I didn't know until recently was that Dr. Williams had developed a personal relationship with Lou Ella and her husband Wallis Wade, but especially with Lou Ella. Rumors of an affair had circulated.

When I became aware of their close connection, I hadn't known that Lou Ella and Dr. Williams had written letters to each other nor that some of the letters still existed. The letters had been included with Lou Ella's papers which had been stored at the law offices of Perkins, Floyd, Davis, and Oden in Alice, Texas, and then somehow, the letters had found their way to my attic.

In the fall of 1926, Dr. Williams was in San Antonio, getting treatment for asthma. He was staying at the Lanier Hotel to be near his doctor, a common practice for out-of-town patients in those days. While he was at the Lanier, he wrote a series of letters to Lou Ella, and she'd kept them for decades, tied together with a blue silk ribbon.

At the time of Dr. Williams' letters to Lou Ella, he was in his 60's, feeling old and broken. His relationship with her had become an emotional lifeline that seemed to tug at his self-reliance. In the letters, Dr. Williams called Lou Ella, "Lady," and she called him, "Doctor." The many underlined words in his letters reveal his intense emotions. He made clear that the place he called "home" was the Big House at the Wade Ranch where Lou Ella and Wallis lived. "No, your letters are not hard for me to read and never too long. Believe when I tell you they are all I get out of life...there is nothing, not anything for me except your letters while here and the thoughts of home yes home"

The letters reflect a man experiencing turbulent emotions and a man depending on one woman for support. "If I could lay my head on your knees and just cry my heart out, that I would either get well or die, and I would not care which . . . Oh how I have longed for you, but I know you could not give up everything and come to me. Still how my poor heart did ache for my Lady nurse." His pain and his difficulty breathing had him considering his own death and reflecting on his inadequacy as a father.

He wrote to Lou Ella, "I have never realized until I came up here what a complete failure [that] I have made . . . out of raising my three children. . . Be sure that you tell Kenny S[labach] to cash no more checks without I sign them . . ." The Doctor was especially vexed by Walton:

> If Walton was a son who had any respect for me or my feeling, he could have got him a cot and put it in here with me. When he would lay down, he would put his feet up at the head of the bed, and every time I would move, he seemed to be mad and wanted to know why I did not relax and get sleep.

Adeline presented a different challenge to her father. She'd married again after Tom had died. The marriage was not going well, and Dr. Williams had been writing to Adeline's husband, Lou, infuriating her. In one of the letters, Dr. Williams described this involvement for Lou Ella:

> I had a long letter from Adeline in answer to the one I wrote to Lou. It was smoking hot with hell and damn in it. Made her mad because I wrote to Lou I guess, but I am used to her by now. Think I will not send the letter I have written as it is sure hard. Think I will just write her a nice little letter and surprise her. She is expecting me to blow up and give her hell, but I think I will just fool her once.

Lou Ella must have been aware of the doctor's

personal problems with his children. His youngest daughter, Mary, relied on Lou Ella and wrote to her about Adeline, "She has no children, only she and Lou, and if they can't manage, I can't take up their burden." The doctor doesn't mention Mary in any of his letters to Lou Ella, but he doesn't think that any of his children are responsive to his needs. He wrote to Lou Ella, "None of my three children care what becomes of me. That is hard to say, but actions speak louder than words sometime."

Lou Ella was the only person he could rely on, and he didn't hesitate to tell her specifically what he wanted:

> Lady, did you ever write for that Bigel
> [Beagle] book?

> Lady, if you can think, bring the blood
> pressure instrument. Just take it apart and
> drop it in your case, it will not break.

> And I wish you would bring my other knife
> and drop a few pecans in your pocket.

Lou Ella also seemed comfortable telling Dr. Williams what he ought to do. He wrote to let her know he'd followed her advice: "I stopped at the R & S and got me the overcoat that you thought so nice. Sure did hate to pay $30.00 for it, but I thought you wanted me to have it because it will last the rest of my life." Dr. Williams willingly took Lou Ella's advice, but he also gave it. He reverted to his professional expertise when he advised her about her father's illness:

> ...but if I was well, I would do all there is to try
> to get Dr. Watson to come out twice a day and
> see him.
> Your father does not need so much medicine,

but he should be watched very close, and try to keep him comfortable. I wish Dr. Watson would wash his stomach out and see what is the matter with him. I think it is ulceration of the stomach. It might be cancer, but I can't think so.

Dr. Williams shared information about his own medical condition. "Dr. Kahn said I had a little pneumonia. I do not think so, though I cough up lots of blood and am still blowing it out of my nose." He followed with even more details:

> . . 8 a.m. Temp 99 ½ . . . I am freezing to death and had a hard rigor, and temperature went to 103" . . . I think the steam heat is responsible for my trouble, as every time it comes on, I go to wheezing, and oncomes a spell of asthma. Had to take three shots last night . . . at 10, 2, and 3.

Again, as the experienced doctor he was, he counseled Lou Ella, concerning her health:

> So why not just wait till [you] come home and then if you want him to operate just come on up here and make one trip do? There is no use to come and be examined, and then go back home and then come again. He thinks the trouble is fibroid tumors, and if that is what it is, there won't be very much danger to it, and that is what I have always thought was the trouble, but we will talk that over when I see you.

He even instructed her on how to keep her chickens well:

Do not feed them anything but mash with Nux Vomica [a homeopathic drug prepared from Strychnine seeds] in it, and don't be afraid of giving it to them. Give plenty of it. The blood of the chickens takes up the Nux Vomica and kills the bugs.

Dr. Williams' letters to Lou Ella also included fun and humor. He joked and flirted with her as if he were a young man:

Made a mark on a good-looking girl this eve, the cash girl at the Medical Arts. She told Walton and another young man who were standing there when I came up to pay for my coke, 'Here is my fellow. He comes to see me every day; ain't he nice though?' And, of course, I told her I only drank the cokes to get a chance to get a look at her.

He found ways to be humorous in the middle of his own unhappiness, describing to Lou Ella, "I am so blue I am black."

The Doctor's relationship with Wallis doesn't show up in the letters very often, but humor and kidding extended to him as well. Only one letter written to Wallis still exists, and it illustrates their bond. When Lou Ella was in Corpus Christi nursing her ailing father, the doctor wrote to Wallis, "I told the Madam in her letter that I wished I was there to help you batch, that I knew we would get everything in a mess, and she would whip us when she came. But we would be willing to take the whipping to have her back home, would we not?"

Fig. 17 Wallis, front porch of the Big House, circa 1930s

The letters of the Doctor to his Lady were written at a vulnerable time for him. At the end of one, he expressed the love he had for both Lou Ella and Wallis, "God bless you both and keep you well and bring everything out OK is the wish of one who loves you both better than a brother."

It could be that he felt his own death might be near: ". . . all I care to live for is just to take care of you all and show how much I appreciate what you have done for me. I know or I feel I owe my life to you all, and there is no one on earth to live for except you two."

❖

When I first heard about the rumored affair between Lou Ella and the Doctor, I'd accepted that the rumors must be true. They were just another sign that Lou Ella always got what she wanted.

But after a second and third reading of the letters, I don't think it matters if the rumors are true or not. The letters show something more than an affair. They show a strong friendship between two tough individuals who've spent their lives fighting for power and position. They've both helped and hurt people along the way, and now he's weak and vulnerable. Lou Ella must have understood this because of her own experience with her dying father. In comforting each other, they found solace.

Who can blame them? Apparently Wallis didn't. And neither can I.

Fig. 18 Wallis and Lou Ella,
Wade Ranch, circa 1930s

Part Two: Almond and Jennie Knolle
1900-1950s

Introduction

I'm one of Almond and Jennie's 12 grandchildren. Nine of us are still living, and we're all still in Texas. We're the only ones left who spent a lot of time with our Papa and Mamaw in their house.

Most of us remember sitting with Mamaw on her living room sofa as we looked through her picture albums. One of them was purple velvet with pansies on the front. Its most striking picture was the one of Mamaw's cousin Minnie Crabb with her husband Thomas and two of their little boys in an old-fashioned open car in front of a grand hotel in Calcutta, India.

Fig. 19 Thomas and Minnie Crabb and sons
Calcutta, India, circa 1898

The other album was gold and green velvet, and there was a picture of Papa when he was two, sitting on a little chair wearing a small bowler hat, a white dress, and black lace-up boots.

Fig. 20 Almond Knolle, 2 yrs., 1877

I feel compelled to tell you about Almond and Jennie. I don't mean the official story that was printed many times in newspapers and in their obituaries. I mean the inner story of their courageous spirits and of the way they gave their lives to each other.

The Bees and the Beauty (1900)

"Louise, I want a safe place for these letters. Will you keep them?"

"Sure, Mama ," I answered casually, and later on, I placed them on one of the shelves in my attic.

Then Mother died, along with most of my Knolle aunts and uncles. And now I am one of the few people left who remembers Almond and Jennie.

The family letters had been kept by Jennie in a drawer with her keepsakes. They range in time from when she and Almond were courting in 1900 through the early years of their marriage, and they continue to around 1930.

Not too long ago out of curiosity, I brought the letters down from my attic and began reading them. They were unlike any letters I'd ever read. They'd been written on cheap paper, sometimes in pencil, and they were honest and simple, telling of rainy weather and attempts to meet at the Lockehill Methodist Church near San Antonio, and later, of bees and babies. Almond and Jennie wrote openly to each other about their fears of not measuring up. And they wrote about their longing for each other. Almond wanted to take Jennie into his arms, and she would write about staying awake, gazing at the moon that was lighting his way home.

The first time I saw my grandparents' wedding picture I felt sad for Almond. His suit is ill-fitting, with the sleeves and trousers too long. One leg appears shorter than the other. His ears stick out, and he looks, well…ugly next to his beautiful Jennie. She's wearing a stylish, lace trimmed wedding dress with a blue sash around her tiny waist. But Almond stands with his shoulders squared and looked directly into the camera. He's 26 years old. He has boundless confidence and ambition and a few bees.

Jennie must have understood him right away. She

later said that she knew from the beginning that Almond was a man who "thought big."

For all his confidence, Almond was in awe of Jennie's beauty. In one of his first letters to her on March 14, 1900, he wrote, "My Sweetheart do you know that I have never seen a girl that dresses as well as you do. Everything you wear becomes you. I believe if you had a dress made out of potato sacks you would still look pretty."

He would write to Jennie about her eyes. "I got to see your pretty eyes so often last night. You have such bright eyes. You dear girl you. I wonder what you are doing now."

And he was unabashedly romantic. "I dream of you every night now and think of you all day. I do not know what I should do if I did not have you to love. You did look so sweet today. I could hardly resist the temptation to take you in my arms just one minute.

And Jennie would answer him:

> I wonder what my dear boy is doing just now? We had such a happy time last night didn't we, dearest Almond, it is going to seem so long to Sunday now. What time did you get home? I lay and looked at the moon for the longest time, I knew it was shining on my darling, as he was going along the lonely road.

Almond's mother had told him if he and Jennie would wait a year to marry, she would sell her property in Flatonia and give him some money. But Almond was in love. He'd thanked her and said, "We can manage on our own." And he told Jennie, "I know my bees can support a little girl like you."

Fig. 21 Almond and Jennie's Wedding Portrait
Lockehill, San Antonio, Sept. 20, 1900

Almond kept his bees on the Donaldson land near Shavano and lived with his mother and sister Buena and his younger brother Lee in San Antonio. Mr. Donaldson offered to sell him some land for $20 per acre, but again Almond turned down a favor. He said to Jennie, "Just wait, we'll buy better land than that."

Jennie agreed with him. She wrote, "It won't matter if we don't have things just "so" at first, for the love we have for each other is worth more than all the gold in the world and I know we will be a thousand times happier than lots of people who have all that money can buy."

Almond wrote to Jennie about bees almost as much as he wrote of his love for her. "Enclosed are a few pages from a bee paper. I used to think the girls on them were pretty. How would you like to hold a swarm of bees in those nice hands of yours? I know you would have won first prize."

Another time he said, "Do you know that a queen bee lays as many as six thousand eggs a day. In the spring they average about two or three thousand." In other letters, he shared details like:

The bees are all right and may swarm soon.

I got a queen bee by mail yesterday.

Am selling over $5.00 worth of honey every day now.

Jennie was eager to share his life with the bees:

How did the honey sell today? I hope you didn't have a hard time, Sweetheart. Never mind though darling, after a while it won't be so hard, for we can both begin and work together...

Once when Almond was at the Donaldson place taking care of his bees, he knew he wouldn't get to church the following week. He wrote to Jennie, "Next Sunday I will be sitting under the trees thinking of you. Such a good Christian a sweet true girl. You will make me such a good wife. Kisses for you my dear."

They'd met at church in Shavano. He wrote to her, "When you were home last summer and I met you at church. The first Sunday you looked so sweet and good I knew right away I loved you."

And, weeks later, "You know darling it will be so much easier now to be Christian."

"Please do not be offended if I speak a little rough and plain. You know I have been running the streets of this city with boys so much. I do not know how to act to such a dear girl."

And, "I'm afraid I have not got as much Christian courage as you."

By that March of 1900, Jennie was 24 and had returned the year before from New Orleans where she'd worked as a governess for the Scudder family. Jennie was the oldest of the five children of Peter and Jane Pearson. Her sister Maggie was 23, and Jennie's brothers, James, Willie, and David were 16, 10, and 3. Jennie's family life became important to Almond.

"Do you know Darling, I love children very much since I became a Christian. They used to try and get away every time I came near."

In his letter of March 14, he wrote, "I picked some wildflowers for you again, my dear. Oh yes, that reminds me of David. I came very close to forgetting him. He showed me his playthings, and he had some wildflowers, and he asked me to smell how sweet. And just think, he will be my brother and Maggie my sister. Such dear relatives your folks will be."

And "Maggie teased me some. She is such a dear girl."

Maggie had a clever sense of humor. She'd tease both Almond and Jennie mercilessly. Jennie wrote to Almond, "Maggie teased me as much as she could before she went, and then she said she would go if I would send you her love. I was glad for her to leave me alone on any terms, but she was earnest when she said it."

Jennie and Maggie were eager to get to know Buena, Almond's older sister. Jennie wrote to Almond, "I want to hear from you before Sunday, and please write and tell me that you will bring Buena. Maggie sends her love and says to tell her to be sure and come if she can."

Jennie's father wasn't as welcoming as the rest of her family. In March, Almond wrote, "I stopped there (at your folks) on the way in today. Your father spoke to me. He was on the way to the field and only said good evening."

That summer, about six weeks before the wedding, Almond suggested, "Maybe I'd better ask your father for your hand. Do men do that now?"

"Some of them do," Jennie had encouraged.

Jennie later recounted that Almond had walked across the field where her father was plowing and asked his permission to marry her. That pleased her father so much that he lent Almond a wagon and team to haul lumber from San Antonio to build their house, along with 16-year-old James to help.

Jennie and Almond married on Thursday, September 20, 1900, at the home of Jennie's parents in Shavano. They were married by the Presbyterian minister at four in the afternoon. Jennie's mother made the white lace trimmed wedding dress. She also fried chicken, made ice cream, and baked the traditional wedding fruitcake with white icing for about 15 guests and family.

Jennie's father gave the couple two cows and two

heifers. Her family from Scotland sent $50.00 for Jennie and Almond to buy sterling silver, but they used it to buy bees instead. Her friend Mrs. Scudder in New Orleans sent them an entire set of blue and white china. Willie gave them a cat.

After the wedding they drove their little wagon ten miles to the new two-room house that Almond had built on the Donaldson land near his bees. It had a kitchen, 4'x6', and the "other room," 6'x12'.

Fig.22 Almond Knolle, Apiarist, near Yancey, Texas, 1906

Almond and Jennie would later tell their children about going to church in the wagon the Sunday after their wedding. When the church service was over, the entire congregation gathered in front to see the newlyweds off. Almond was eager to get away. He quickly helped Jennie into the wagon and jumped in beside her. When he turned to wave goodbye, they heard a roar of laughter. Almond had forgotten to unhitch his horse.

From Hondo to Sandia (1907-1925)

Fig. 23 Mary, 6 yrs., Katherine, 4, Henry, 2
Hondo, Texas, 1908

It was after dark when the train arrived at the Sandia Depot. The family had left San Antonio at nine in the morning and spent two hours waiting in Skidmore for the branch train. Almond was taking Jennie and the three children to see the land he'd bought. Mary was still five, Katherine had just turned four, and Henry was eighteen months.

They didn't plan to live on the land in Sandia. The bees were in Hondo and Yancey. But with an eye toward the future, Almond had wanted to make a good investment.

He knew the land was good because it had big timber on it. He'd paid the lawyer from Seguin, Mr. Dibrell, $20.00 an acre for the 405 acres.

It was August 1907 when the Almond Knolle family arrived in Sandia. Almond and Jennie didn't know then that the land would be in their family for over 100 years. Nor did they know that it would someday be home to the world's largest herd of Jersey cattle.

It might have been hard for Jennie to think about the future. She probably thought about another train ride, the one when she first arrived in Texas. Her parents had brought the family to Sequin from Scotland when she was five, and her youngest sister, two-year-old Katie, and baby George had caught diphtheria on the train, and they'd died soon after. Only she and Maggie, three, had survived.

That had been a long time ago, and now there would have been no time for Jennie to reminisce. Her own family was arriving in Sandia. Her three children were fussy, she was bone-tired, but, as ever, Almond was full of energy, happy they were going with him to their new land.

Jennie must have been relieved to see her brother, Willie, at the depot. He loaded the family and their provisions into a wagon and took them six miles along a cow trail through mesquite brush until they came to the camp where he'd been staying. Willie had set up a tent with some cots for them, and they slept through their first night, "bothered only by a few mosquitoes."

The family camped for a week with Jennie washing their clothes in the river and Almond cooking over the campfire. After a week in the tent, they moved into a barn that had just been built. There were men building houses and barns and clearing brush. Almond put himself to making fences.

Although it was late in the summer, wildflowers were still in bloom. Mary and Katherine played outside on the sandy land. Occasionally, Almond and Willie would take the wagon to Sandia for mail and groceries. The family stayed on the new place for three weeks and then went back to Hondo and the bees.

A few months after they returned to Hondo, Almond and Jennie realized they would have to live on the land to take care of it. Almond sold most of his bees, and in May of the following year, two months after their fourth child, Arthur, was born, the family moved permanently to Sandia. Jennie's parents Jane and Peter Pearson had just moved to Sandia from San Antonio, and Almond and Jennie stayed with them until their own house was finished.

The Pearsons had emigrated from Scotland in 1881. By the time they moved to Sandia, they'd lived in India, Scotland, New York, Boston, Seguin and the Lockehill community in San Antonio. In later years, Jane would often tell her children and grandchildren that she had lived all over the world and everywhere she lived she'd been lucky to have wonderful neighbors.

Peter Pearson was hardworking and ambitious. By the time he was 25, he'd worked for 11 years as an accounts clerk, and at 29, he took a position in India managing a coffee plantation where he injured his right hand in a shooting accident. After arriving in Sequin, his first work was making coffins for his two youngest children. He blamed himself for coming to Texas and causing the deaths of Katie and George. He became depressed and bitter and never adjusted to life in Texas. Peter had to pick up whatever job he could find. He farmed, sold pots and pans as an itinerant peddler, he was a carpenter, and in Sandia he was a blacksmith.

*Fig. 24 Peter and Jane Pearson, Bangalore, India, 1875.
Peter lost 3 fingers on his right hand in a gun accident in India.
In this portrait, his hand is concealed by a glove.*

Jennie and Almond moved into their new home in July 1908. Bob, Ed, Ruth, and Walton were born in the following years.

Fig. 26 Watermelon Season, Sandia Depot, circa 1909

Sandia grew into a prosperous town. There were seven grocery stores, two hotels, a telegraph and a telephone, two banks, two drugstores, a jailhouse., a cotton gin, two scales and a blacksmith shop. But Mary remembered the South Texas weather. Years later, she wrote to her father, recollecting hurricanes that had come through, "Mama and all of us stood by a back window watching you tie down the windmill....I remember waking one calm sunny morning after a hurricane and finding the kitchen half full of chickens Mama was trying to revive."

In the 1920s, the Sandia Depot was an exciting place. In one year, 556 carloads of watermelons were shipped out. Classes at the Sandia school lasted seven months each year, ending in April when cucumber and watermelon season would begin. The Knolle brothers worked at the depot loading watermelons, some of which weighed 80-90 pounds, nearly as much as the younger boys.

Fig. 25 Foreground, Arthur, 8 yrs., with a pigeon on his head, and Bob, 6, holding a kitten.
Background, Ed, 4, and Ruth, 2
Knolle farmhouse, Sandia, Texas, 1916

The area boys of all ages found other exciting things to do. At one point, Henry and Arthur saw a magazine advertisement about "Farmer Burns School of Wrestling." Henry later wrote, "we put a few dollars of our possum and coon money together and ordered the nine monthly lessons..." Meetings of the boys ensued. "Those who attended were Jim, Charlie and Tommy West, Arthur, Bob, Ed, Walton, and Henry Knolle, Jack Kring, Watson Cockhran, Bert Williford, Zack Pruett, Ernest Miller, and Bob Almond."

Wrestling and fighting were serious business for the Knolle boys. Bob used to tell a story about "the big fight." He remembered when Henry and Arthur, about 14 and 12, fought for over an hour on the screened porch. They turned over milk cans and the separator. When the fight was over, eight or ten pans of milk that had been ready to skim were all on the porch floor. "Mama couldn't stop'em," Bob said.

According to Ed, Arthur had the first radio in the family. It must have been one of the early crystal radios common in rural homes in the early 1920s. It could pick up a signal without electrical power, but earphones had to be used. Arthur would share his radio with his brothers by using one of the earphones himself and turning the other earpiece, so the second person could hear. Arthur lent out half of his radio on the condition—the borrower had to pay by doing all Arthur's chores for one day.

Fig. 27 Pig feeders, Bob, 8 yrs., and Henry, 12
Knolle farmhouse, 1916

All the children had chores. When Almond was in Yancey checking his bees, he wrote to Jennie, "The boys can feed the cows about 1 quart of cotton twice a day…if it is too hard to get the moss, they can get Juan to help get a wagon load and take it there to feed…Tell them not to get kicked or hurt climbing."

By 1922, the two oldest Knolles, Mary and Katherine, had begun their teaching careers and were helping the family with parts of their salaries. They stayed close to their littlest brothers and sisters through letters. Ten-year-old Ed wrote to Katherine in Robstown, sharing details of his days:

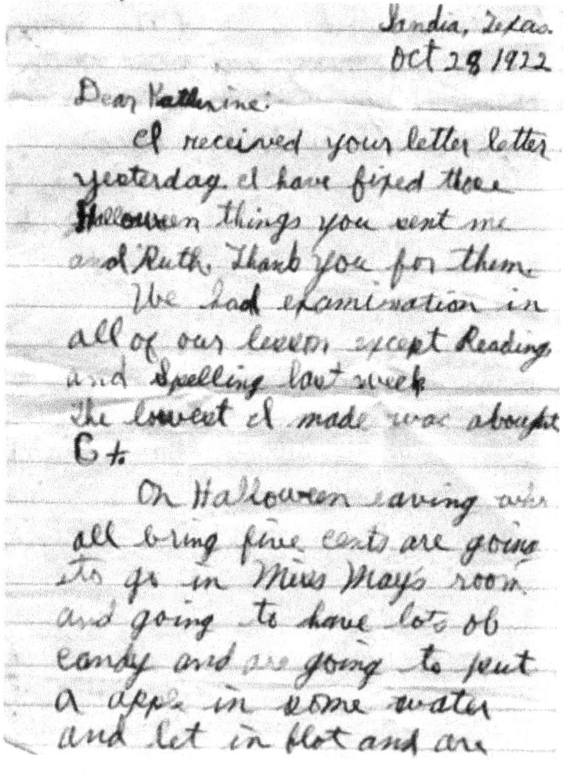

Fig. 28 Ed's letter to Katherine, page 1
Oct. 28,1922. Ed was 10 yrs. old

Dear Katherine,
I received your letter yesterday. I have fixed

the Halloween things you sent me and Ruth. Thank you for them. We had examination in all of our lessons except Reading and Spelling last week. The lowest I made was about C+. On Halloween evening who all bring five cents are going to go to Miss May's room and going to have lots of candy and going to put an apple in some water and let it float and are going to put our heads in and see who can get the apple. When you touch it will go under ... Ruth is sick in bed this morning. Arthur and Henry, and some of the West boys went hunting last night and caught a wildcat.

Love from Edward

Once in 1923, when Ruth and the five brothers were still all in school in Sandia, a small airplane landed on the school ground. A blonde, lanky young man climbed out of the plane and, as the crowd of children gathered around him, offered to take anyone up in the plane for $1.00. Arthur rode their horse home to get the money, came back with one dollar, and was the first in the family to go up in a plane. In later years, the brothers decided among themselves that the tall blonde stranger must have been Charles Lindberg. It's true that Charles Lindberg had been barnstorming in South Texas during those years, and it's also true that the $1.00 plane ride shaped Arthur's lifelong love of flying.

Arthur hadn't even been born in 1907, when the family had made that long train trip to see their new land in Sandia. Soon, with Henry at Texas A&M and Mary and Katherine away teaching, Arthur would be the oldest child at home. In 1925, the youngest five Knolles would begin another adventure, from Sandia to the Sparkling City.

The Sparkling City (1925-1930)

Mamaw's living room was old even back then in the early 1950s. Although there were lots of windows, it was always dark and cool. There was a spinet piano, a bookcase built by Papa, and two rockers, a soft one for him and a hard, wooden one for her. The sofa was deep and squashy.

I remember when I was eight and spending the afternoon with Mamaw and Papa. Mamaw was telling me about old times.

"Louise, did I ever tell you about our first trip to Corpus after we moved to Sandia?"

"Yes, Mamaw. But tell me again. It's my favorite story."

"Well, one summer day, Papa and I decided we wanted to take the family on a vacation to Corpus. We went in a covered wagon and camped along the way. It took us two days to get there."

I settled down into the sofa. Mamaw leaned forward. Her back was still straight.

"And Mamaw, where was my daddy?"

"Your daddy and Ruth and Walton weren't even born yet. Bobby was just a tiny baby."

I knew the story well. "And what did you eat?"

"We had a picnic. I'd baked bread and made fried chicken and stacks of cookies before we left home. The wagon was loaded with feed for the horses, so we slept outside on mattresses."

"Were you scared, Mamaw?"

"I was never scared when we were with Papa. I knew he would always take care of us, wherever we were. The next day we rented a little cottage on the beach, and every day we ate pink ice cream and went swimming two times."

Papa interrupted us from his rocker over near the

radio cabinet. "Is Jennie still as beautiful as she used to be, Louise?" I laughed, "Yes, Papa, she's still beautiful." Papa was blind, so he couldn't see Mamaw, and he always asked me this. Mamaw was so old there was no way she could be beautiful to anyone except Papa. Even though I was only eight, I knew how much they loved each other.

I realize now how much Papa did take care of them. He and Mamaw raised five boys and three girls on their farm near Sandia. Not one of their children ever had a broken bone or a rattlesnake bite.

Fig. 29 Walton, 2 yrs., Katherine, 15, and Ed, 6
North Beach, Corpus Christi, Texas, 1918

Papa would constantly watch the weather. In early September 1919, the family was again vacationing on the beach in Corpus. I'd heard later that he'd seen a "queer haze" and had quickly packed them all up and headed back to Sandia. Hours after they'd arrived home, a hurricane hit Corpus Christi without warning. The 1919 Hurricane was one of the worst coastal disasters in Texas history, killing from 600 to 1000 people.

❖

In 1925, six years after the hurricane, Jennie and Almond moved to Corpus to be near good schools for the five youngest children, Arthur, Bob, Ed, Ruth, and Walton. By that time, Henry was in another town, and the two oldest children, Mary and Katherine, had left home to become schoolteachers. Ruth was the only girl among the five youngest siblings. She would later say that her worst experiences in Corpus were when Ed made her walk behind him every day on the way to school because he didn't want the other kids to know she was his sister.

Fig. 30 Walton, 8 yrs. Ruth, 10
In front of the Corpus Christi house, 1207 6th street, 1925

While they were living in Corpus, Ed's job was to milk their cow daily and take a quart of fresh milk down the street where he'd sell it for a dime. He and Papa kept the cow staked in a vacant lot.

One summer Ed opened a hamburger stand near the

newly opened Port. He cooked the meat right out in the open, and the hamburgers sold quickly to the hungry workers. Ed made money by using day-old bread and hiring his fifteen-year-old friends. Ed's younger brother, Walton, liked hanging around the burger stand. One hot afternoon, Walton slipped a cupful of red ants into Maurice Nast's pants while he was making burgers for Ed. Years later, Maurice became a prominent physician in Corpus, and although their paths crossed many times through the years, Dr. Nast never forgave Walton.

Fig. 31 Arthur Knolle, 1927

Arthur was the athlete of the family. In his 2 years at Corpus Christi High School, he played football, basketball, and ran track. His friends called him Artie.

There's a family story about Bob and the flagpole sitter. Bob had heard about a flagpole sitter who was about to set a world record in Corpus, so he decided to play hooky from school to watch the event. When he arrived downtown, there was a big crowd gathered, but Bob was lucky. A few people let him stand right in the front because of his small size. The next day Bob wasn't so lucky. A reporter from the *Corpus Christi Caller* had brought a camera along, and there on the front page, right next to the flagpole, was Bob for all to see, including his teacher and the school principal.

Soon after they'd moved to Corpus, Bob had gotten a job delivering newspapers, but he hadn't liked it and had quit. Bob went on to get a job making banana splits at a drug store, not knowing he should cut the bananas lengthwise instead of in half. Bob sold his second-hand bike to Ed, who went and asked Mr. Floyd for Bob's old job delivering papers.

"A kid with your last name took this job and quit after one week. Do you have any cousins, son?"

"No sir. I don't have any relatives," Ed replied.

Ed got the job and kept the paper route for two winters, quitting only in the summer to get a full-time job. He folded papers early in the morning with his friend, Wallace Dinn. At that time, neither of them could've imagined that Wallace would become a local war hero when his plane was shot down twice over the Pacific in World War II.

When Ed had worked for the Corpus Christi Caller, he'd been allowed two free newspapers each day. He would bring one home and would usually sell the other. Often, he'd let an old lady at the end of the route have the last one. One day in 1926, she was outside, waiting to get the paper from him. She'd said she wanted to read about "the murder case."

The murder case was the trial of Harry Leahy, a 39-year-old bachelor who was an attorney from a prominent family in Mathis. Harry Leahy had lost his land, and he'd blamed the loss on a Mathis physician, Dr. J. A. Ramsey. There had been bitterness and a shooting between Leahy and District Judge W.F. Timon over the land matter. One evening, making up a story that his sister was sick, Harry Leahy sent his hired hand to get Dr. Ramsey to come treat her. Dr. Ramsey started out for Leahy's house, but was instead kidnapped and killed by Leahy in a grisly murder that made headlines all over the country. The hired hand escaped to Mexico but was later apprehended. He confessed that Harry Leahy had ordered him to help torture and kill Dr. Ramsey. Leahy was tried and sentenced to life in prison. His lawyers appealed the case but lost. Harry Leahy was then sentenced to death, and he died in the electric chair in 1929.

During the years of his paper route, Ed developed a deep interest in the news and learned his way around Corpus. He became familiar with the downtown area and the variety of activities that took place there. The Nixon Cafe was a gathering place for people working downtown. The Cafe was in the Nixon Building which was said to be the first skyscraper in Corpus. Ed and his oldest brother,

Fig. 32 Ed, 13 yrs. old
Front porch of the Corpus Christi house, 1926

Henry, often saw Lyndon Johnson meeting at the Cafe with his Democratic Party associates. Years later, after Johnson had risen to power, Henry remarked to Ed, "It's too bad we didn't know Johnson was going to be President, we could've gone into the Nixon Cafe and made friends with him."

The years in Corpus Christi from 1925 until 1929 had changed the lives of the young Knolles. They'd gone from a world bounded by muddy roads and mesquite brush to a world bounded by the sky and the sea. They'd gone from lamplight and hauling water to a world of electric lights and indoor plumbing. They'd gotten their first telephone.

The young Knolles grew up in an air of limitless opportunity.

Okra and Nasturtiums (1948)

I'm a picky eater. I like oranges and tomatoes and milk and fried chicken, but mostly I like birthday cake and ice cream, and Mamaw's plain cookies.

I'm happy today. I'm going across the road to have lunch with Mamaw and Papa. Their house is fun. Cousins are always there, and Papa teases us. He'll tease Mamaw too, about her brothers. He'll talk loud when she's near the room, and tell us, "Scottish people are pessimists—just look at Uncle James and Uncle Willie." Papa is German, and he says he's the only optimist in the family. "A pessimist is just a pest," he'll grin. But Papa never calls Mamaw a pest. He just smiles at her.

Mamaw has probably fixed fried chicken for me today. Whenever we have fried chicken at home, I ask my daddy Ed why he always takes the wing. He tells me about the eight Knolle brothers and sisters crowded around the table for Sunday dinner. They'd all grab for a piece of the chicken that Mamaw had just killed, plucked, and fried. Daddy always took the wing. He still does.

Lunch is ready when I arrive, and no one else is there. I don't smell any fried chicken either. I go with Mamaw and Papa into the kitchen and see the table with three plates and three chairs. It's a special lunch, just for the three of us.

Mamaw's plates are very old. I know she and Papa got them when they married. The plates have green and orange food on them. "Come sit here, Louise. Look, we've fixed you food from our garden. Okra and nasturtiums!"

I try to smile. Why are they giving a lunch like this to a girl who's a picky eater? Mamaw's proud the nasturtiums are still bright orange. "Look Louise, they're the only flower that's good for you to eat. Aren't they pretty?" She moves the plate closer to me. There are bumpy blue lines on her hands.

I take a teeny bite of the orange flower, and I get a plan. I'll smile a lot, nod my head, and just take little nibbles. Mamaw and Papa don't say anything. They must think I like the food okay.

"The okra is from our garden, too. I'll go pick some and show you," Papa says. He gets up, and I see him hold his hand along the wall when he leaves the kitchen. He makes his way to the garden and comes back with a bunch of okra. I've never seen okra before. Papa leans over the table toward me and hands me the okra bouquet. "Take it home to your Mama," he says.

After a while, Mamaw gets up from the table and comes back with a plate of big cookies for dessert. I drink all my milk and eat four cookies. It's a good lunch after all.

All of a sudden, I know Mamaw and Papa are old, even older than the plates. And I know I love them.

Fig. 33 Mamaw and Papa on the Nueces River
Joe Knolle, 5 yrs., in the right foreground, July 4, 1951

Papa Shows Me His Bees (1950)

Mamaw places the small box on her dining table. "Look, Louise. This just came for Papa in the mail."

The box is small enough for me to hold in my hand, and it has a piece of screen for the top. And there's something moving in it. Papa must've heard her because he comes into the dining room right away. His cane taps loud, and his face has a big smile.

"Is my queen here, Jennie?"

"Yes, I just went out to the mailbox. She's finally here!"

Mamaw gives him the box. She looks over at me.

"It's a queen bee, Louise. Papa's been waiting for her to get here."

She sits down at the table and goes back to snapping green beans. Papa puts his head close to the box. "It looks like she's made the trip just fine." I look into the box, too. I don't understand how a bee can take a trip in the mail.

"How did the queen stay alive in the mailbox, Papa? Did the mailman take care of her?"

"He didn't have to," Papa grins. "Worker bees come along to feed her and take care of her. See, they're in here, too. And here's some of the leftover food." He points to some crumbs in the box. "They've come all the way from California."

"Where's California, Papa?"

"It's a state like Texas. Queen bees can travel a long way. I've sent bees to other countries, even to Australia."

"Is Australia as far away as San Antonio?"

Papa sets the box on the table and laughs. He kneels down on the worn-out floor and puts his hand on my shoulder.

"Australia's a lot farther than San Antonio. It's

even farther than Scotland. Right, Jennie?"

Mamaw smiles at him. Her hands keep snapping beans, and Papa keeps talking.

"Louise, do you want me to show you my bees? Tell your daddy to bring you to the Bee Pasture this afternoon."

"Oh, I will! Where's the Bee Pasture, Papa?"

"It's right next to the River Pasture. Your daddy knows all right."

"Will we take the queen with us?"

"No, she has to rest here for a while, but we'll see lots of bees."

It's afternoon now, and Daddy's driving me to the Bee Pasture. All at once, I remember the bee that stung my brother in our backyard last year. Charles was only five, and that bee really hurt him.

"Will the bees sting me, Daddy?"

"Just stay with Papa. He'll take care of you."

Daddy always says Papa is careful with little kids. I take a deep breath and lean back in the seat next to Daddy. Soon he says, "Here we are at the Bee Pasture."

I get out of Daddy's old Buick and wave as he drives away.

"I'll be back in a little while," he calls. "I'm going over to check the heifers at the River Pasture as long as we're over here."

Papa makes his way through the brush with his cane. He holds out his hand.

"Here, come with me, Louise."

His step is strong as he leads me down the path to his beehives, and I forget he's almost blind. Papa's at home with his bees.

"Papa, what if they sting me?"

"They won't sting you, Louise. Just be nice to them and they'll be nice to you. But here, take my hat. It'll make you feel better."

From one of his pockets, he pulls out an old felt hat, all folded up. He unfolds it, and I see the brim of the hat has net hanging around it. He helps me put it on. I'm happy. I'm wearing a bee hat, and the bees can't get me through the net. And even if they do, Papa will take care of me.

"But Papa, what will you wear? Won't you get stung without your hat?"

"Don't worry about me with bees, Louise. They like me. They know I'm good to them. But now, we have to get to work. I want to check everything before we leave."

I watch Papa pull the frames of bees from the hives and clean the little honey house. He tells me about the queen and the workers and the drones. He shows me the honey the workers have made.

"Look, Louise, some honey has dripped onto this frame."

He scrapes up some honey with his pocketknife. "Take some with your finger and taste it." I take the honey from the knife and lick my finger. It tastes just like the honey Mama puts on my toast, only sweeter.

Some of the bees are buzzing around Papa's face. They get on his jacket, but they don't sting him. I pull the bee hat down and get closer to the hives. I try to be good to them like Papa.

After a while Papa says, "I guess I'm about ready to go, Louise. Why don't we head toward the road and meet your daddy there?" He takes the bee hat off my head and begins to fold it. As we start down the path, I wonder what Papa was like when he was eight.

"Did you have a grandfather, Papa?"

"You bet I did. I had two of them. One was named Bernard Scherrer. He came to Texas in 1849 from Switzerland. He became an Indian fighter and a friend of

Sam Houston, the leader of the Texas Revolution. Bernard Scherrer was a scout for Sam Houston, and he helped Houston defeat the Mexican general, Santa Anna.

Fig. 34 Bernard Scherrer (1807-1892)
Biegel, Texas, circa 1840's

"My other grandpa was the first Knolle to come to Texas from Germany. His name was Ernst Friedrich Gottlieb Knolle." Papa says the name slowly and really loud. "He settled in Industry, Texas in 1844. He grew cotton and owned a cotton gin, a lumber mill, and a flour mill. My Knolle grandpa worked hard and made a lot of money, but he was a Confederate and lost all his money during the Civil War.

Fig. 35 Ernst Friedrich Gottlieb Knolle (1812 - 1880)

"His children were hard workers, and they all did well. I had a lot of cousins. Six of them became doctors, and that wasn't easy in those days. It was my cousin Willie Gehrels who got me started in bees. He gave me my first hive before I even met Jennie, and I've had bees ever since.

"Willie's the only one in my family who likes bees. Sometimes, I wish one of my sons was interested in bees. Your daddy and your uncles all like cows. Jennie likes cows, and my mama always had a cow. None of them understand that bees are less work and more fun. A lot of people would feel lucky to get a chance to help with these bees."

"Maybe I can help you when I get big Papa." He leans over, and his rough hand touches my face. "I wish you could, Louise. I wish you could."

We hear Daddy driving up. I run to the end of the

path. Papa follows.

"Daddy, I got to wear Papa's bee hat! And I tasted the honey the workers made. And it was good!"

I turn around. "Thank you, Papa. This was fun." I stand on tiptoe and put my arms around him.

Daddy leans out of the car window. "Can you get home all right?"

Papa straightens up against his cane. "Of course, I can."

Tea with Mamaw (1952)

"Tea? I don't like tea. Do I have to go?"

Mama puts her hands on her hips. "Yes, you have to go, and yes, you have to wear your new plaid jumper."

"Will there be a lot of people there?"

"Louise, it's okay. It'll be fine. It'll just be you and Mamaw."

I get out of the car and wiggle my jumper straight. I'm only 10, and my mother has me dressed up and ready for tea.

I give my grandparents' front door a quick knock and then go ahead and open it. I see Papa sitting in his big chair in the living room. He's listening to the news on his radio. I go over to him and take his hand that's resting on the arm of the chair.

"Hi Papa, it's Louise." I give him a kiss. He always likes for us to kiss him now that he's blind. He leans forward and turns down the volume on the radio.

"How're you doin', Papa?"

"I'm feeling pretty good, Louise. I think I can see better today. If I look over there, I can see some light." He turns his head toward the front window. He knows the window is there, in the same place it's always been.

"That's good, Papa." He smiles and turns toward me.

"Optimistic, Louise, it's the only way to be." I feel proud. He's so brave.

"You better go on in there and see Jennie. She's been getting ready for you. Having tea is good," he whispered, "but I wish I had a beer." I pretend not to hear. We grandchildren aren't supposed to know Papa likes beer. But I know a lot of things because I can keep a secret. I go through the door to the dining room.

"Oh Louise, I'm glad you're here." Mamaw's eyes twinkle, and she gives me a peck on the cheek.

Mamaw's dressed up too. She has on her black lace-up shoes, not the ones with the toes cut out. She's putting two blue and white plates on a little table. She's set up the card table between her big dining table and the old wood-burning stove. She never cooks on the stove anymore, even though it's still there. My daddy always tells me how she would keep a pot of hot chocolate on it in the winter.

"Louise, we have to move this table back right after we have tea. I try to keep the furniture in our house exactly the same, so Papa won't bump into things." A tablecloth with lace is on the table. Two dining chairs are on either side. Two places have been set with napkins and spoons and forks, and there's a sugar bowl and a little pitcher of milk.

Mamaw motions to the built-in cabinet in the corner of the dining room. "Come over and look at my collection of teacups. You can choose the one you like for your tea."

I've seen her cups and saucers, and I know some of them are very old. They're on the top two shelves of her cabinet, and they look like they'd be easy to break. They have designs and flowers on them.

On the shelf below the cups and saucers are some strange looking cups with men's faces. One's a man with a fancy hat, and I could see the dark brown collar of his coat. Another's wearing a gray fisherman's cap, and he's got the face of an old man with a beard. I like the fisherman best, and I'm about to choose him. But I see Mamaw looking at a dainty teacup with pink roses on it, and I know she wants me to choose that one.

"I like this one with the roses." Mamaw gives me a pat on the shoulder. She's happy I've picked her favorite.

"Here, take the cup and saucer over to the table,

and I'll get the tea."

I've just placed my cup on the table when Mamaw comes from the kitchen. She has her blue and white teapot and her own matching cup and saucer. She sits down with her back as straight as ever. I sit down too and try to hold my back straight.

'We're lucky to have this rich Jersey milk for our tea." She pours the hot tea and a little milk into the two cups.

"And now, Louise, add two teaspoons of sugar. I think you will like it if it's sweet. It's important to remember, you should never add lemon to your tea." Before I can ask the reason for the no-lemon rule, Mamaw disappears into the kitchen again. My hand shakes, but I put in the spoons of sugar without spilling. The tea is warm and sweet and milky. Then I learn the best thing about having tea.

"Back home in Scotland we never had tea without some sweets to go with it." Mamaw puts down a blue and white plate with some of her big plain cookies and little pieces of cake.

"Oh Mamaw, did you have tea like this every day?"

"Why yes, I guess we did. Sometimes we'd add a little meat with it and call it 'supper,' but just tea and toast with honey can make a good little meal."

I reach for a big cookie with one hand and a piece of cake with the other. I'm thinking Scotland must be a good place to live if they have tea every day.

"Tell me about Scotland, Mamaw."

"Well, I was born in India, and my parents didn't take me back to their home in Scotland until I was almost two. And then, we moved to Texas when I was five, so I don't remember much about it. I do remember how cold it was when our family walked across the moors on our way to church. They wrapped a big wool scarf around my head, and I could barely see."

Fig.36 Jennie Pearson, 2 yrs., Aberdeenshire, Scotland 1877

I giggle. "I bet you looked cute. Did your family always walk to church? Did you have a big family?"

"We walked a lot. I remember the fresh smell of heather in the fields. It's a little purple flower that grows everywhere in Scotland. My mother had lots of brothers and sisters, so I still have many relatives in Scotland, aunts and uncles and cousins."

"Did any of your relatives move to Texas with you, Mamaw?"

"No, none of my aunts and uncles and cousins came with us, only my mother and father and we four wee ones. I was the oldest and next was your Aunt Maggie. Then came poor little two-year old Katie. And there was baby George, my parents' first little boy. Katie and George both died as soon as we got to Texas."

I sit up straight. "Oh Mamaw, what happened?"

"Well, when we first got to New York, we stayed in a boarding house for a few days and then took the train to Boston. Papa got work there. It was hot compared to Scotland, and Mama had to cut up her linen tablecloth to make dresses for us. Then, we got on another train to St. Louis and then on to Texas. All four of us children caught diphtheria on the train. Katie and baby George died."

It's so sad I don't know what to say, so I just look down. We're quiet for a little while.

Mamaw finally starts talking again. "Maggie and I were sick, too. I was afraid that Maggie would die after Katie, and then I would die last because I was the oldest."

All I can say is, "Oh, Mamaw."

She gets up from the table quickly and says, "I'll bet you'd like another cookie, Louise. Let me get a few more."

By the time she comes back, I have another question.

"I know you were born in India, Mamaw. Was Aunt Maggie born in India, too?"

"No, Louise. About a year and a half after I was born, there were threats of uprisings in India, so my parents decided to return to Scotland."

"What are uprisings?" I take another cookie.

"They were afraid the native people of India would fight the British people there and try to run them out. My father didn't want Mama and me to get hurt, so he stopped managing the coffee plantation and took us home.

"I was two by the time we got to Scotland. We had to cross the Suez Canal on the way back. A few years before, my father had been on the first ship that ever went through the Suez Canal with passengers."

"What's the Suez Canal?"

"I'll tell you what, why don't you help me put up

these dishes and move the table back, and I'll show you Papa's scrapbook of the Suez Canal."

We put everything away, and I go with Mamaw to a cabinet on the other side of the dining room. She opens the cabinet door and bends over.

"Here it is. Mama made it for him many years ago."

The scrapbook is huge. Mamaw puts it on the dining table, and we sit down to look at it. We open it, and it covers the end of the table. The pages are thin and a light brown color. I can tell the book is very old. She shows me pictures of Egypt and of the Suez Canal being built for the ships. I turn the pages slowly, so they won't tear.

"Do you ever wish you could go back to Scotland, Mamaw?"

She looks out the dining room window, "Of course, I'd like to see my family again, and I think I must have inherited my father's love of travel."

Mamaw's quiet for a little while. As she turns her face back to me, she smiles, "Those times are gone now, and I have Papa and all of you. But I still write to my cousin in Scotland, and I like going to Mexico."

I hear my mother knock quietly on the front door and tiptoe into the living room. She must guess Papa's asleep in his big chair. Mamaw and I look up from the book as she comes into the dining room.

"Louise, it's time to go. Papa's asleep." She sees us with the book and says softly, "Oh Mamaw, I'm so glad you're showing Louise your scrapbook. It's time she learned something about our family."

Getting up from the table, I try to be quiet, too. "I like having tea, Mama."

I turn toward Mamaw and give her a kiss. I whisper, "'Bye, Mamaw, I had a wonderful time."

"So did I," she whispers back. She smiles at me, and her eyes return to her scrapbook.

Part Three: Some Stories 1950s-1970's

Introduction

Fig. 37 Easter 1948, Eight Knolle Cousins
L to r Carolyn, Charles, Pearson, A.W., Ginny, Louise, and
Susan

It was Easter Sunday, and I was six. Most of us cousins lived right near Mamaw and Papa's house, and we were there to hunt eggs and have our pictures taken. Kathy was still five, and I remember her yellow dress and her straw hat with a green ribbon. Mother had fixed my hair in braids on top of my head, and I felt grown up holding baby Susan.

The boy cousins wore little suits. That was the Easter my brother Charles had pink hair. He'd fallen out of the car and scraped his head, and the Mercurochrome that Mother put all over the scrape had turned his blonde hair pink. All of us cousins thought it was funny that a boy would have pink hair.

Mamaw and Papa's house was white with a green roof. The flowerbed next to the front porch was bright with pink and blue hydrangeas from Easters past. That Easter Mamaw sat on the front porch swing holding Susan in her lap facing her. Mamaw loved babies and would give each one her undivided attention, saying, "We just couldn't ask for a sweeter baby."

Papa liked to play with the boys. He would tickle them, and roll them in the grass, and help them find eggs. He would hug us girls and laugh while watching us play with our new pet bunnies. It was only a few years later that he began to have trouble seeing. He thought it was from a splinter that flew into his eye when he was chopping wood. He liked chopping wood and would say, "He who chops his own wood warms himself twice." But it wasn't a chip of wood. It was glaucoma, and Papa became blind.

In Part Three of this book, I've wanted to share what the days were like for us cousins on the Farm. And I want you to know my brother Charles, my aunts Katherine and Ruth, and the five women who married the five Knolle brothers. You'll find a story by my aunt Mary, the first of Jennie and Almond's children, in the Appendix.

I'll Always Have My Cousins (1953-1954)

In the late 1960's, Carolyn and I spent a summer living in the same apartment complex in San Antonio. Carolyn was in the middle of her divorce, and mine hadn't yet begun. One day the two of us were on the way to North Star Mall, when, out of the blue, Carolyn remarked, "You know, Louise, I never feel like I need friends because I know I'll always have my cousins."

After I divorced and was living with my children in Corpus, I realized what Carolyn had meant. Carolyn and I were two of the 12 Knolle cousins, and we all knew we'd had an incredible childhood. Carolyn and I've agreed that our memories have sustained us. We've had heart-rending experiences in our middle years, divorces, the loss of loved ones, and the death of dreams. Whenever we're discouraged and depressed, Carolyn and I've remembered the stories we cousins have shared that have nourished us.

We aren't proud of all our cousin stories. I remember with dismay the time at our mothers' Hub Club celebration at a friend's house in Mathis when I was seven. We cousins went into a bedroom and barricaded the door by piling chairs in front of it. I can still see the two oldest boys, Pearson and A.W., stacking chairs and a small table in front of the door and quietly motioning for us to do the same. We cousins just wanted to play by ourselves like we always did.

And some of our memories are really frightening. One time, A.W. dropped some gravel into a pan of sulfuric acid that was behind the Farm office. The acid splashed up into his eyes. A.W. would've been blinded, but Mrs. Gallagher, the office secretary, saw him and hurried to wash his eyes out, and now his eyes are as good as ever.

We still talk about Pearson getting run over when he was just three years old. His father Henry was driving their car slowly in the driveway with Pearson sitting on the front fender. All of a sudden, Pearson jumped off the car to go see his mother, who was hanging clothes on the line. Pearson ran right in front of the car, and Henry ran right over Pearson, who ended up between the wheels of the car. Pearson stayed down long enough for the car to run completely over him, and when he finally got up, all he had was a little bump on his head. The stories all run together as I remember the summer of 1954 when we ranged in age from 6 to 12.

❖

Our parents want us cousins to learn Spanish, so Mama's decorated our front porch like a classroom. She's hung serapes, posters, maps, and sombreros. A Mexican teacher who lives on our farm comes twice a week. She's 16 and is very pretty with shiny dark hair. Her name's Minerva, but we call her Minnie.

We cousins are having a busy summer. We're going to have a circus for Ginny's birthday, Kathy and I'll be a tap dance team, and we already have matching outfits. Charles and A.W. are going to be clowns.

Fig. 38 A.W., 12 yrs., and Charles, 10, The Circus, 1954

Ginny's going to do trick riding on her horse, Starfire. She has a cowgirl outfit, and she can hold one arm in the air and lean way over to one side on the saddle while she's riding. I think Susan will be a tightrope walker. She's so little, they're going to put a rope on a bench and let her walk on it that way. Joe will be a snake handler, probably with rubber snakes. I don't know what the rest will do. It's going to be in Carolyn and Susan's yard. All the aunts and uncles will be there, and Daddy's going take movies. Last year, Daddy built a pool for us on the riverbank. We'd already learned to swim in the river and in the swimming lessons we took together at Chase Field last year in Beeville.

Fig. 39 Chase Field Swimming Pool, Beeville, Texas, 1953
Charles, 9 yrs., Kathy, 10, Louise, 11, A.W., 11, Carolyn, 10

And now, we have a real swimming pool. The Pool is 45 feet long and made of rough concrete. Daddy built it to be part of our Farm's irrigation system. He pumps water out of the river into a huge pipe that winds up the riverbank, but before the river water goes to irrigate the pastures that feed our cows, it goes through our swimming pool. We share the Pool with fish and frogs and sometimes a water snake or a snapping turtle. They come up the pipe. Overhanging oak trees drop leaves and small branches into the Pool, but the trees make it cool and shady, so we don't mind pulling leaves out of the water.

Fig. 40 Our Pool at the Farm, 1953
Pearson, 11 yrs. and Charles, 9

Sometimes our grandfather, who's blind, paddles in the shallow end. Our aunts, Mary and Katherine, help Papa get into the Pool. They're both schoolteachers, and before that, they helped take care of their six younger brothers and sister, so they're used to kids. Mary and Katherine stand straight and tall in their old-fashioned swimsuits, keeping an eye on Papa and watching us play. They love us cousins, and they bring us good presents from their trips to Europe.

Papa likes children and doesn't mind the splashing water. His eyes haven't improved, although he tells us he thinks he can see a little bit better every day. He listens to books, ball games, the news. and weather reports from the cabinet radio in his living room. He walks a mile or two every day, and he's worn a path next to the picket fence in his front yard. I pray every night for Papa to be able to see.

Fig. 41A Ginny, 8 yrs, and Carolyn, 9, at the Pool, 1953

Fig. 41B, Louise, 11 yrs., and Kathy, 10, 1953

For us girls, the best part of the Pool is all the water coming through the big pipe. It's our own waterfall, cool to stand under, dive under, and push each other under. Kathy, Carolyn, Ginny, and I spend hours giggling and telling secrets under the pounding water, hoping it'll make us skinny. We're always hoping something will make us skinny. Kathy thinks we should try to be like Esther Williams, so we girls practice water ballet a lot. We're trying to learn to float on our backs and kick our legs up in the air without sinking and choking. When we learn how, we'll get in a circle and do it to music. One time, Kathy tried so hard to kick her leg up that she sank, and we thought she might have drowned. But she came up laughing. Kathy always comes up laughing.

We want a diving board, but we know better than to ask for one. Our parents think they're too dangerous. I can't see why our parents won't let us have a diving board in the Pool when they let us cousins ride all over the Farm on our horses. Sometimes we meet at the pool on horseback, but we can't go swimming if parents aren't there.

Last Christmas, Charles and I both got horses. Mine's a little bay mare, short and kind of fat. I named her the most beautiful name I could think of. Spanish Dancer, Dancer for short.

Dancer has a rough trot, but when she lopes, we get along nicely. At the same time, Charles got Lucky Boy, a handsome Palomino. Lucky Boy is famous. He used to be owned by Cactus Jack, a TV Cowboy who led the Corpus Buccaneer Days Parade on Lucky Boy. Charles practiced a lot on Tony, our gentle Shetland pony, and now he can ride Lucky Boy standing on the saddle.

Fig. 42A Charles, 8 yrs.
On Tony, our Shetland pony, 1952

Joe and Pearson have a sorrel horse named Dan
Their father Henry always names their horses Dan.
Sometimes Charles and Lucky Boy meet Joe and Dan at
the Pool. Dan is hard to control, and Joe rides half off of
the saddle, barely hanging on. Joe must be lucky because
he's survived riding Dan. Our parents have let us continue
riding, even though we've had accidents. When Susan was
four and on the way to the Pool with Carolyn and Ginny,
she fell off Pepper, had a concussion, and was blind for
eight hours.

Like Joe, Margaret is 10, but she's not as lucky.
Last year, she fell off her horse and got hurt bad. She had
to have an operation and have her spleen removed. Mama
says having a spleen isn't all that important, but I think it
must be, or we wouldn't have one. Margaret was

determined to get right back on her horse El Gato and she started riding again as soon as they'd let her.

Fig. 42B Thomas Lain, 8 yrs.
Corpus Christi, 1956

Margaret is one of the Lain cousins. Janice, Margaret, and Thomas live in Corpus and come to the Farm every summer to stay with our aunt Katherine. This summer they all have gardens. Janice has planted a flower garden with zinnias, marigolds, bachelor buttons, and periwinkles. She even has sweet peas growing up the fence. Thomas has vegetables in his garden: tomatoes, okra, peppers, cucumbers, and a big watermelon they're going to eat soon. Margaret had big plans for flowers, vegetables, and some hay for her horse. But she hasn't done any of the work, and her garden's just full of weeds.

This afternoon the whole family has had a picnic at the pool after swimming. But now everybody's gone home but us. Charles is down at the river with Daddy turning off the pump, and Mama's putting the last of the picnic stuff in the car. I'm back in the Pool, floating, and the water's gentle and cool. It's almost dark. I tighten up. In just a few weeks, I'll be in the 8th grade, my last year before high school. I don't know what it'll be like. So I think of my cousins. My neck and shoulders soften, and the water feels safe.

I've felt that way so many times in these last difficult years. Remembering all these stories of my cousins, the Pool and the circus and the sunny days on the Farm have lifted and upheld me.

As Long As We Can Remember (1954)

My mother Mary Margaret likes to tell me the story about her first Christmas on Knolle Jersey Farms after she married my father Ed Knolle. It was 1938, and she was 17. The Knolles had gathered at the house where their parents, Almond and Jennie, lived. Almond and Jennie had moved into the house in 1908, and later it was known as the Home Place to their three daughters, Mary, Katherine, and Ruth, and their five sons, Henry, Arthur, Bob, Ed, and Walton.

It's hard for me now, in my forties, to imagine my young mother on the Farm as a newcomer. Arthur and Grace had married a few years earlier, and later, after the rest of the Knolle brothers married, the five sisters-in-law developed great camaraderie.

My mother's first Christmas Eve with the Knolles was at the Home Place where everyone had gathered to decorate the family Christmas tree. They were industriously trimming the tree when Bob nudged Arthur, "Remember that Christmas Eve when we were little, Arthur? We went with Henry and the dogs to hunt for a possum, and we came back early and saw Mama and Papa laughing and decorating the tree together."

"Yeah, I remember that. And do you remember when Henry used to move you to a different bed after you went to sleep, and then he'd tell you the next morning you'd been sleep-walking?"

Everybody laughed, and Mary Margaret, trying to join the fun, threw a handful of icicles on the tree. The laughter stopped, and they all glared at her. Ruth leaned forward and whispered, "You're supposed to put them on one-by-one, Mary Margaret." They all laughed again.

More Christmas Eves went by, more marriages, and 12 children were born within six years of each other.

Fig. 43 Christmas Tree, the Knolle Home Place, 1939

Pearson, A. W., and I were the oldest of those 12 children. Nine of us cousins lived on the Farm near Sandia and played together every day. The other three cousins lived in Corpus and spent summers on the Farm.

For as long as I can remember, all of us Knolles have gathered at Papa and Mamaw's house on Christmas night, and our other grandparents come too. My Nana comes, and Ginny's grandmother Mrs. Huvar is there. Janice's grandmother Mrs. Lain and Kathy's grandmother, Mrs. Beall sometimes come. In the living room, straight-backed chairs line the walls to make places for the adults. We cousins just run around.

Fig. 44 Kathy, 3 yrs., Janice, 2, Louise, 4,
Christmas night at Mamaw and Papa's, 1946

The party begins when one of the cousins stands by Mamaw's piano and reads the Christmas Story. After that, one of the adults says a long prayer. Our aunt, Katherine, takes her place at the piano, and we sing Christmas carols.

And for as long as we can remember, Mamaw gives each of us cousins a book with a special note inside. Papa gives us a wrapped silver dollar tied with a red ribbon. We take turns going to his chair to thank him.

Papa has been completely blind for several years now. When we thank him, he holds our hands and looks at us as if he can see our faces. Last Christmas, he noticed a ring on my left hand. He stiffened and leaned toward me.

I laughed, "Oh no, Papa, don't worry. I'm only 15. I won't be engaged for a long time." He leaned back and grinned.

Pretty soon, we cousins are ready to move on. We like to see each other's presents, so all the aunts, uncles, and cousins go around to the Knolle houses on the Farm. At each place, the presents have been arranged under the tree, and we cousins rush to see them. There's food at every house.

The first house in our Christmas caravan is my cousin Ginny's. My aunt, Adele, has placed her homemade divinity on dainty china plates in the dining room. My uncle, Bob, holds court at the kitchen table with a glass of whiskey. He's driven all the way to Luling to get his special sausage. We eat it on paper napkins. Bob likes to talk about football, "If A&M and the Devil were playing against each other, I'd be for the Devil."

Right across the road from Ginny's is Carolyn and Susan's house, so we walk over there. My uncle, Arthur, always hangs Christmas lights on the big cedar tree in front of their house. The colored lights twinkle in the Christmas air. Once inside, I push my way to the table where my aunt Grace's English creams are placed. They're a creamy mixture of caramel and chocolate, and I eat three pieces and hope no one notices.

Then we go to Pearson and Joe's house. Their place is a few minutes down the road, so we drive there. All of us girls want to go together, but we can't all fit in one car, so Susan and Margaret have to go with my aunt Grace and uncle Arthur. Susan and Margaret are mad, but Grace pretends to cry and soon has them laughing.

Pearson and Joe's house has a big dining room set off from the rest of the house. The dining room resembles a stage, so we have our performances there. A few years ago, we put on a play called "Christmas on the Farm 1920." Mama wrote it, and we cousins played the parts of our parents and grandparents. I'm the oldest girl, and I got to be Mamaw. I wore a long skirt, and Mama arranged my hair in a bun just like Mamaw's.

The play began perfectly. But a scene halfway through the script called for Pearson and Joe to be backstage at the same time. The brothers started fighting, and Joe refused to go back onstage. Everything fell apart, and the play just ended.

Our caravan moves on. At A.W. and Kathy's house, my uncle, Walton, gets out the Mogen David wine for the grown-ups, and we have my aunt Dorothy's fudge. Dorothy makes the best fudge. She's given me the recipe, but I haven't ever made it. Whenever I want to make it, Mama shoos me out of the kitchen, saying, "Louise, you go outside with Ed and the cows. You'll have your whole life to be in the kitchen."

Now we are finally at the last house, mine. It looks beautiful. Mama lets Daddy and Charles and me put up the tree, but she likes to decorate the house. She puts lights and green branches everywhere, and last year, she put a big letter to Santa over our fireplace. The letter was made of a sheet of wrapping paper, and the writing was all in red and green glitter. It said, "Dear Santa, we have been good all year. Love, Louise and Charles."

At our house, we eat Andrea's tamales. Every year, Andrea washes the shucks until you can see light through them. She'll show me the shucks in front of the kitchen window and say, "See Luisa, this is how you tell a good tamale."

We Knolles are now exhausted. All of us girls go to my room to listen to my new Rock 'n' Roll records. The boys invade Charles's room. They're playing with his new toys, and I bet they'll all be broken by morning. The grown-ups are in the game room, sipping eggnog with their feet up. Their laughter trickles down the hall.

Fig. 45 Christmas 1953
Front Row, l. to r., Carolyn, Ginny, Joe, Susan
Back Row l. to r. Charles, Pearson, Louise, Margaret, Thomas,
Janice, A.W., Kathy

Our last Christmas Day with Papa was in 1968. He was 93 and had been sick for many weeks. His bed had been moved to the dining room, and we cousins gathered near him. He couldn't sit up, but he still managed to take each of our hands as we shuffled around the bed in a circle to greet him. He pressed my hand firmly, and he whispered, "Louise, how are my orange trees looking?" My eyes filled with tears. "They're lookin' good, Papa." And I moved away to make room.

The Cruelest Month (1903-1984)

Two things happened that week in April that I've always connected in my mind. Katherine died, and our main calf barn burned down.

Katherine was my 81-year-old aunt, and she was going to be buried in our family plot in Sandia. As I drove past the burned barn on the way to Katherine's funeral, tears ran down my cheeks. Ninety-six baby Jersey calves had burned to death in the fire that morning.

Fig. 46 Katherine, 44 yrs.
holding her niece Margaret, 18 mos., 1948

Katherine had loved all kinds of babies. She visited Geordie when he was only weeks old. Geordie was a teeny, bald baby. Katherine had carefully braided her hair and put on her navy and white visiting dress. As she sat holding Geordie, her body was still and straight, but her face was soft.

Katherine was an affectionate "Nanny" to us 12 cousins, but I didn't understand her complexity and courage for many years. She could have been beautiful. She was tall and slender with the fine angular features of her Scottish forebears, but she didn't seem to have much interest in the surface of things. She'd valued intelligence, independence, and relationships. Katherine had grown up in a time and place that offered few choices for women, yet she'd quietly and creatively lived her life outside the boundaries of what was expected of her.

She was a schoolteacher in Robstown by the time she was 18 and immediately began to help her family. A story about Katherine takes place in 1928. The story goes that Papa was about to lose the farm because he didn't have one hundred dollars to pay the mortgage, so Katherine, Ed, and Papa went to a bank in Corpus to try to get money. Katherine went into the bank building alone while Ed and Papa waited a long time in the family's only car.

Finally, Katherine returned with the hundred dollars she'd borrowed on her teacher's salary. Papa just grinned and shook his head, "Ain't that a miracle!"

In the 1930s, Katherine began traveling to Mexico, and she and my aunt Mary took her mother Jennie to Mexico City. In 1935, Katherine took a bus tour across the eastern U.S. and into Canada, and she wrote home from Salem, Mass,. "I do wish all of you would draw the line at doing so much work. Have been thinking all along the trip how ideal a vacation for about four of the family to take about the same route we are and stay at little tourist camps which are much nicer looking here than at home." She continued, "The native shrubs here and in Canada are not the same as in Jim Wells County. Have seen so many pretty, yellow-breasted robins since I left."

Until I went off to SMU in 1960, Katherine and my aunt Mary were the only people I knew who had spent time in Europe. I still have the dainty cream pitcher Katherine brought home from their 1949 trip. It's from Bavaria and has a hand painted Little Bo Peep and a clumsily translated version of the English nursery rhyme, "...leave them alone and they'll come home, and bring their tails behind them."

Katherine's life was filled with more drama than was visible. She'd had secrets that were never explained to me. I'd heard that Katherine had one great love in her life, and after she'd lost him to another woman, she chose never to marry. As a child, I hadn't understood why Katherine had abruptly quit her 30-year teaching career and moved to the Farm. I'd heard grown-ups talking about a "nervous breakdown" and how it would be good for Katherine to come back home.

Katherine had owned 200 acres of land with a creek running through. When Katherine moved back, her brothers Ed and Henry helped her build a two-bedroom frame house and a dairy barn for milking about a hundred cows. She'd named her place Creekside Farm after one once owned by her Scottish ancestors. Whenever I'd visited Katherine, baby calves would be playing in her front yard, and I'd heard that some of them spent cold winter nights in her kitchen.

Katherine had had a long career as a teacher, beginning right out of high school. Later she'd gotten a degree at the University of Texas and taught high school in Corpus. She'd been my mother Mary Margaret's history teacher, and Mama had always valued Katherine's judgment. When I was 18 and planning for college, Mama had suggested I talk with Katherine for advice, "Katherine will be the best person for you to talk to about choosing your major, Louise. Go by and see her."

So, I'd gone to see Katherine at her house. She and

her little dog Honey greeted me at the front gate. She gave me a brief hug, and soon we were sitting side-by-side in front of the fireplace in her wood-paneled living room. Katherine's coffee table was littered with travel books, farm magazines, assorted mail, a sock, and at least three used coffee cups. The living room opened into a small kitchen with a sink full of dishes and several large calf bottles, all needing washing. Black rubber boots were at the screen door.

"Louise, if you're interested in business, begin by reading the business section of Time magazine." It was great advice. The Time articles were so boring to me that I rarely finished them. And my first business courses at SMU were equally boring. I quickly changed my major to liberal arts.

Katherine, like all of us Knolles, had enjoyed riding around the Farm to see what was going on, to see the weather, and to see what shape the fields were in. During her years at Creekside Farm, Katherine had faithfully taken her aging parents on daily and dusty rides, and sometimes they'd stop at the Knolle Store. One blistering August day in 1970, I'd walked out of the store and seen Katherine in her little gray car. Katherine was still in her khaki skirt and cotton blouse from working all morning and was taking her mother on her daily ride around the Farm. Katherine had leaned out of the window to say hi. I went over to give Mamaw a kiss, and we talked for a minute about the hot weather. As they'd driven away, I was overwhelmed with sadness. Katherine had lived a well-traveled and creative life, and now, she was alone with only her mother, looking for someone to say hello to in our old store.

Now as I look back on that scene with more years and more wisdom, I know that Katherine had lived exactly as she'd wanted. She was able to live on her own through her later years, and she continued to drive her mother around each day. They liked to check out the weather and the cattle in the fields. At dusk, Katherine could go home to Creekside Farm to feed her baby calves.

Fig. 47 Katherine, Ruidoso, New Mexico, circa 1950s

Five Knolle Women (1931-1996)

I was on the phone with John, telling him that Mama was ready to go home, when a loud buzzer sounded, and a nurse rushed in.

"Do you want to resuscitate?"

"What do you mean?" Suddenly the room was crowded. The nurse leaned toward me and lowered her voice.

"If she dies…"

"Oh no, we don't want her to die! Do anything you can."

Daddy was standing in the corner of the room, arms folded, and eyes wide open. The phone was still in my hand.

"John, they're asking me if I want them to resuscitate."

"I'll be right there."

A crowd of nurses appeared and ushered Daddy and me out into the hall. I knew immediately I'd done the wrong thing. Mama and I had talked several times about her wishes, and she'd signed a living will. Daddy and I stood helpless and quiet.

A friend passed by and greeted me cheerfully. I blurted, "My mother's in there. I think she's dying." My friend seemed embarrassed to have intruded, gave me a brief hug, and walked on.

Suddenly John was there. He stopped the procedure. And then it was over. Mama was dead.

I called Charles. He wasn't home, so I told Beth. I called my best friend, and she called our priest. Father Bruce was there in what felt like minutes. He spoke to Daddy and me briefly, and Bruce and I went into Mama's room. Daddy stayed out in the hall. Bruce opened the *Book of Common Prayer*, and we prayed the Anglican "Prayers at the Time of Death." I felt comforted by the familiar words, but I could see Daddy was still standing alone out in the hall.

I left the room and went over to him. "We should go home now. Charles will be there. Is there anyone you want me to call?"

"Call Florence."

Fig.48 Florence Mahoney Knolle 1940

I felt a wave of relief. I knew we'd get through this all right. Florence always knows what to do in times of trouble. Just a week ago, Daddy had called to tell me Mama was in a lot of pain. I'd rushed right over, but Florence was already there, talking quietly to Mama and rubbing her back.

Why hadn't I thought to rub my own mother's back? Florence is strong, and she always does the right thing.

Daddy and I left the hospital and made the trip back home to the Farm. Florence and Henry were waiting in the dark on my parents' front porch. We all hugged. I knew immediately that Florence wasn't going to be strong for me. Her tall willowy body seemed to have shrunk, her beautiful hair, always pulled neatly back, was frizzy, and she moved tentatively.

"I just can't believe it," she kept saying, over and over. Henry was looking as helpless as Daddy. I thanked Florence and tried to comfort them. I told them to go home and get some rest.

Fig. 49 Mary Margaret Buchanan Knolle, 1938

Mama and Florence had been close for several years before Pearson and I were born, nine days apart. They had helped raise each other's children and helped bury each other's parents. They'd chosen the same China and crystal patterns, so they'd have enough matching dishes to properly entertain cattle people from all over the world.

Mama and Florence were two of the five sisters-in-law, who'd married the Knolle brothers and lived near one another on the Farm. Now Mama and Dorothy had died, and Florence, Grace, and Adele were left.

Fig.50 Grace Davis
at the Sandia Schoolyard, circa 1931

Grace and Mama had known each other longer than any of the others. Their relationship went back to Mary Margaret's school days when Grace taught the 11-year old budding writer. Grace had noticed Mary Margaret's talent and encouraged her to enter the Ready Writing contest at the Jim Wells County Meet. Grace took Mary Margaret to Alice where Mary Margaret wrote an essay on "What Does Our Flag Stand For?" They came back with a first-place ribbon, and Mama kept that crumpled blue ribbon in her jewelry box for 65 years.

The Knolles say that Arthur heard about Grace— the pretty new teacher from Hillsboro—and wanted to meet her. So, he landed his plane in a field next to the Sandia schoolhouse and offered to take the Sandia schoolteachers up for a ride. Grace married Arthur a few years later, and he taught her to fly. Grace got her license and became one of the first women pilots in Texas. Mama took lessons from Arthur, too, but she'd married Ed, and before she could solo, he made her quit flying.

Grace may have had the grit to fly solo in those single-engine planes, but she also had a warm charm about her. I remember when Grace would arrive late at the Mathis gym to watch high school basketball games. Her daughter's boyfriend was a star player on the Mathis team. She'd get there long after the bleachers were packed and stand near the Mathis Pirates' benches. Pretty and helpless, she'd gaze up into the bleachers for a spot. And she always got a front row seat.

In those years there was a popular dance hall in Tynan, a small farming community north of Mathis. Once a month the hall had a strictly monitored dance for the teenagers in the area. Before Kathy and Carolyn and I were allowed to date, Mama, Grace, and Dorothy would drive 25 miles to take us to the Tynan dances. We'd carefully stuff ourselves into the back seat of my parents' Buick sedan, trying not to crush our full cotton skirts and petticoats.

After every dance, Kathy and Carolyn and I would find our three mothers laughing at some private joke. Waiting in the car for us was their chance to be together, free of husbands and children.

On the ride home we'd give them a full report, who was there and who we'd danced with. We'd tell them about every funny thing, like the boy who was too shy to ask the pretty Carolyn to dance. He'd go right up to her and then quickly turn his back and walk away. Billy Pickens was a boy who liked Kathy. His mother, Mrs. Pickens, was in charge of keeping order at the dances and making sure that no one went out to the parking lot. She kept a constant eye on Kathy and Billy.

I remember so much from those good times, but now, most of all, I remember Dorothy's laughter. When Dorothy laughed, the world became happy. I loved being with her. She'd grown up in the old Lagarto community near Mathis, and everybody in Mathis was her friend. Dorothy had a tiny waist, a petite figure, and wore fashionable dresses. She had a sharp, quick wit and read constantly. Dorothy was a member of the Mathis Literary Club and liked romantic novels and movie magazines. Her daughter, Kathy, spent lots of whole days at our house, and it was great for me. We'd go down to the store and get Byerlys soda for 5 cents. Then we'd go down to the silos across from my parents' house and sell them for 10 cents. Kathy and I knew we were lucky to get to spend so much time together. Much later in my 50's, I understood why.

Dorothy was fragile and was often unhappy, and Mama would try to help her. She and Dorothy spent a lot of time together, shopping and talking about books and children. Dorothy's moodiness must have begun early. After A.W was born in the spring of 1942, Mama wrote to her mother:

Fig. 51 Dorothy Beall Knolle
with A.W., 1942

When we got back from S.A., we found that
Dorothy had gotten sick and gone to her
mother's to stay 'a month'...the doctor says it's
nerves. Anyhow Walton has had enough of the
getting up at night, I think.

I know now that Dorothy may have had postpartum
depression which was not understood to be an illness then.

*

Fig. 52 Adele Huvar Knolle,
Picnic at the River, 1941

Of the sisters-in-law, Adele was the last to come into the Knolle family when she married Bob. She was a brown-eyed blond and had a straight, slender figure. Adele remained exactly the same size she'd been on her wedding day. She attributed her slender figure to the glass of hot water she drank every morning upon rising.

Adele adored Bob. She'd been a schoolteacher in Garland and later taught in Sandia and Mathis. Adele lived her life carefully. She cleaned one kitchen cabinet every day, so the cabinets were always neat and she'd never have to clean all of them at one time. She and Bob stayed all their lives in the same house they'd moved into as newlyweds, and she thriftily saved her teacher's salary.

Adele and Bob had one child, Ginny, and her birthday was always marked with good parties for all the cousins. For Ginny's first or second birthday party, we played a fishing game. I didn't know what fishing was, but I knew that Adele was behind a big sheet and that if I put my string over the sheet, Adele would attach a little toy to it. I remember spending the night with Ginny a few years later and seeing Adele's glass lamps in the spare bedroom. I thought those lamps with pink roses painted on them were the most beautiful lamps in the world.

These Knolle women, Mary Margaret, Florence, Grace, Dorothy, and Adele, had made decisions when they were young to marry the five Knolle brothers. By chance, they became sisters. Their enjoyment of each other's company kept the Knolle family close. Kathy once remarked to Carolyn, "You know, I could never get away with anything because I had so many mothers watching me."

A Tall Ship and a Star (1960-1997)

We were sitting at my kitchen table, and I could hear the wind rattling the shutters on my front porch. Anxiety washed over me as the norther blew in.

"But Charles, you have a reputation for calm, good judgment. People respect you."

"Not anymore, Weegee. I've lost a lot of my credibility."

Charles hadn't been so open with me in a good while. He and Debbie had spent years on his Westsail 32, *Fata Morgana*, sailing in the Caribbean and along the East Coast. A few years ago, he'd divorced Debbie, married Beth, and come back to live on the Farm with Beth and her two young daughters. He was being honest about his situation, and I was relieved he was confiding in me. But his elbows were on the table with his face resting in his hands.

"Oh no, Charles. You haven't lost any credibility with the people who really know you."

I'd protested too much. We both knew his alcoholism had cost him. Charles got up from the table and went outside to smoke. When he came back, I was unloading the dishwasher and had the teakettle going. The phone rang. It was Beth, and he left.

I fixed my tea and sat back in my chair at the kitchen table. The hot tea warmed me, and I began to gather things for the chicken soup I'd planned for supper. I thought about how different our lives had become. Charles and I had always found shelter in one another, but now in our mid-forties, everything was different.

Charles had returned to a place that had changed dramatically since he'd left 18 years earlier. He'd spent four years at SMU, one year at law school, one year in the Navy Reserves, 12 years in the Caribbean, only coming home for brief visits. After he moved back to the Farm, he seemed disoriented, as if caught in a world where he no longer belonged. His memory of the Farm was still one from his experience as a 19-year-old.

When Charles left for SMU in 1962, hundreds of workers had lived on Knolle Jersey Farms in homes provided for them and their families. By the time Charles returned in the 1980's, life on the Farm had changed. Now, instead of living in housing owned by their employers, many families had moved off the Farm and built their own homes nearby. Women living on the Farm now wore jeans and worked and earned money like their husbands.

After our brief conversation in the kitchen, Charles and I saw each other again a few weeks later. It was Thanksgiving, and I had come to my farmhouse with my children and our German shepherd, Belinda. My parents and Charles and his family were there. I was at the back door, trying to get Belinda out of the house when he came down the back hall. He could see that I was worried about her being in the house.

"It's okay to have a dog in your house, Louise. Belinda's a good dog."

I knew Charles understood that I was trying hard to please our father. Ed was a conservative dairyman critical of anybody who would allow animals in the house.

"Thanks, Charles."

I was relieved and let Belinda back in. Belinda followed him back into the living room, tail wagging. I stayed there at the door for a few minutes, thinking about all the times Charles had comforted and helped me.

We'd both gone to Southern Methodist University in Dallas. The first thing I'd done there was get bumped out of sorority rush. The photo I'd naively sent as my introduction to the sororities was of myself with a Jersey cow. It hadn't impressed anyone.

*Fig. 53 Charles, 17 yrs., and his dog, Rebel,
with Charles' first sailboat, FJ584, 1961*

Two years later, Charles had arrived at SMU with a brand-new Buick Riviera that had black leather seats and a portable TV in the back. My father had given it to him, and it'd been the best car on a campus full of rich kids.

Charles was blonde and good-looking, a golden boy for whom everything seemed possible. He'd been president of his fraternity, and he'd learned to drink. Charles and Lynn had fallen in love and married before they'd graduated from college.

One time I'd gone over to their apartment to study for an exam in Dr. Covici's class on the American novel. Pascal Covici was a romantic figure, tall and dark with a pipe and a well-worn tweed jacket. Charles and I were in Dr. Covici's class together, and he was our favorite teacher.

"Charles, what am I going to do about the exam tomorrow? I haven't even read *The Red Badge of Courage*."

"Just look through the book quickly, Weegee, and look over your notes. I can tell you about it."

He'd first read the book while still in high school. "You see, Henry's wound wasn't a red badge of courage. To him, it was a red badge of shame."

On the exam, I'd written down exactly what Charles had told me and made an A. Charles hadn't even cared and had made a C.

Charles learned easily and did everything with a nonchalance that was both impressive and irritating. I remember one time when we'd been home together in our mother's kitchen. I'd given him a hug and said, "I used to be smarter than you, Charles, but now you've outgrown me." He'd smiled and changed the subject.

Charles read, he traveled. He liked good music, good food, and good friends. His specialty was steak and kidney pie. He'd always loved the Farm, but his great love was the sea.

Charles' first boat had been a rowboat he'd made out of an old wooden feed trough. He named the boat *El Dorado*, and he floated down the river in it. By the time he was in high school, he had his own sailboat, a 13-foot fiberglass dinghy that he sailed on our lake at the Farm. I'd been his first crew. The winds were strong and erratic, and it was a chore to keep the boat upright. Charles taught himself to sail by reading about it and practicing on that little lake.

Charles's dream had been to be an officer in the Navy. When he'd applied for Officer Candidate School after college, he'd been surprised to learn he was colorblind. They'd let him take the color test three times; each time he'd failed it, and he'd been turned down for the Navy OCS. Within the next year, he and Lynn divorced. Soon after, Charles's best friend and sailing buddy, Bill Best, died in a car wreck a few weeks before he was to retire from the Navy as a Captain. This triple blow changed my brother's life.

By 1973, he and his sailing companion, Debbie

Bennett, left for the Virgin Islands on *Fata Morgana*. Charles told my father that the trip would take about a year. Twelve years later, they returned to the Farm. [See Appendix 5 for Charles's reminiscences about that long period at sea. Also see the poem, "With Mrs. Columbus in Mind."]

Charles developed a serious drinking problem. He'd blacked out several times on the boat and had gone to a doctor in Houston who'd warned him he had to stop drinking. I talked to Charles about his health at that time. "Charles, what will you do? Will you go to AA?"

"No, I can handle it myself."

Soon Charles divorced Debbie and married Beth, and they were living on the Farm. Our parents had supported him and believed in him for years, but at that point, problems developed. His relationship with them and with me was soon over.

Plagued by alcoholism, Charles died of throat cancer one day before his 54th birthday.

Ruth's Story (1915-2002)

"What will Ruth get into next?" was the attitude of Ruth's five brothers. She'd been the youngest girl in the Knolle family, surrounded by her brothers. They'd always thought girls were just for teaching school and raising children. And Ruth had confirmed that opinion, becoming a teacher and having three children.

Daddy was two years older than Ruth. During the years she was teaching, they'd often had heated arguments about teachers' salaries. I suspected they'd always argued about something or other. The fact that Ruth had worked hard all her life, had had a happy marriage with LeRoy, and raised three grown, successful children didn't matter. Ruth was a girl.

Ruth was fun and creative, more my friend than my aunt. Once she told me about how, when my parents had first married, she and Mama had scandalized the rest of the family by sunbathing on the roof of my parents' house in full view of the main road to Sandia.

Ruth and I were sitting on the floor in the attic bedroom at my house. We'd been doing some stretching exercises together and now we were just relaxing and talking.

"Louise, why don't we take a yoga class together?"

"Oh, Ruth, I wish I could take a class with you. But with Geordie and the new baby and the work I do out here, I just can't take on one more thing."

"Well, I've been watching "Lilia's Yoga Show" on TV and following along with her in my living room. I think I'd like it, and I'm going to try to find a class to take."

Ruth had been trying lots of things since she'd retired from teaching English at Carroll High School in Corpus. Most everything she'd tried was related to health. Recently, she'd been selling Shaklee products. But that was beginning to bore her. Ruth had had a hard time as a young girl. When she was very small, she'd had the measles, a devastating disease in those days. Ruth survived, but the measles left her with poor eyesight and one crossed eye. She overcame this physical handicap and graduated from the University of Texas. She'd taught school for 33 years.

Ruth had married LeRoy Lain when she was in her twenties, and they'd raised three children, Janice, Margaret, and Thomas, in a house full of love and laughter. From my visits there, I remember the all-you-can-eat pancake breakfasts and the boa constrictor that Thomas kept in his shower. Piano music, and piano noise, was ever-present in the house as Ruth and the three children all played the piano with varying degrees of skill.

When Ruth began looking for a yoga class, she was 65. And there were no classes in Corpus. She came up to my house one day with a new book, Richard Hittleman's *Yoga 28 Day Exercise Plan*. "This guy is really good, Louise. I'm going to work with this book a few weeks, and then I'll start going to workshops. There's one next month in Dallas."

Ruth was a natural teacher, so she decided to have her own class instead of waiting to find one to join. And Ruth found her calling. She continued to teach and practice yoga daily until she died at age 87.

When the Knolle brothers first heard about their sister's new venture into yoga they were puzzled. Who ever heard of such a thing? Was it a food? A religion? And where was it from? India? Why would a person want to do something from India?

Finally, they became exasperated. "Why does she spend so much time on 'that yogi stuff'?" "Isn't that just like Ruth?"

Fig. 54 Ruth Knolle Lain, 85 yrs.
Downward Dog

Meanwhile, Ruth was becoming a legend in Corpus Christi. She was helping hundreds of people find self-respect and meaning in life through yoga. And they grew to love her. She was a patient and understanding teacher. Her headstands, her sun salutations, and the bounce in her step at age eighty inspired them.

Ruth's yoga teaching was noticed on a national level. There were articles about her in yoga journals, and she was pictured in the latest yoga books. But the thing that finally got my father's attention was a three-page spread with photos of Ruth in the *Corpus Christi Caller*. I showed it to him at our office one morning before work. A grin slowly emerged on his face as he read the article about her. He didn't say anything to me. He rushed out with the paper to where the workers were gathering, and I followed. I watched as he went up to each tractor driver and each mechanic. He showed them the newspaper, "See this, this is **my sister**."

When she was 87, Ruth was told she had advanced ovarian cancer. She lived only weeks longer. I visited Ruth in her hospital room soon after the diagnosis. She was in pain and her joints were stiff. She eased herself out of the hospital bed, all bent-over, to creep into the bathroom. She got halfway there and stopped. I watched as Ruth slowly raised her body and straightened her back. I imagined what she was thinking. Ruth planted her feet firmly and lifted her head as if pulled up by a string into Tadasana, the Mountain Pose. She paused for a moment and glided the rest of the way.

Part Four

Knolle Jersey Farms
Stories from 1951-2013

HOME OF THE
WORLD'S LARGEST JERSEY HERD
SANDIA, TEXAS

Located 32 miles west of
Corpus Christi, Texas on Farm
Road No. 70.

HOME PLA
Barn

THE JAVALINA

RED BARN
Charles and Louise Knolle Jerseys

4 MILES TO ORANGE GROVE

30 MILES TO KINGSVILLE

HIGHWAY 70

CHAPARRAL FARM
Barn No. 8

R. E. KNOLLE DAIRY

FORT LIPANTITLAN

FARM TO MARKET ROAD NO. 1833

WALTON KNOLLE FARM

FARM TO MARKET ROAD NO. 624

BLUNTZER ROAD

KNOLLE JERSEY FAR
Barn

RANCHO VERDE
Barn No. 7

SALT CEDARS
Barn No. 9

28 MILES TO CORPUS CHRISTI

10 MILES TO SAN

138

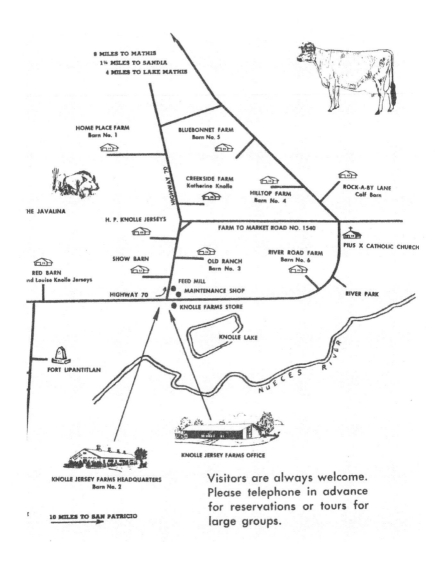

8 MILES TO MATHIS
1¼ MILES TO SANDIA
4 MILES TO LAKE MATHIS

HOME PLACE FARM
Barn No. 1

BLUEBONNET FARM
Barn No. 5

HIGHWAY 70

CREEKSIDE FARM
Katherine Knolle

HILLTOP FARM
Barn No. 4

ROCK-A-BY LANE
Calf Barn

'HE JAVALINA

H. P. KNOLLE JERSEYS

FARM TO MARKET ROAD NO. 1540

PIUS X CATHOLIC CHURCH

SHOW BARN

OLD RANCH
Barn No. 3

RIVER ROAD FARM
Barn No. 6

RED BARN
and Louise Knolle Jerseys

FEED MILL

HIGHWAY 70

MAINTENANCE SHOP

RIVER PARK

KNOLLE FARMS STORE

KNOLLE LAKE

NUECES RIVER

FORT LIPANTITLAN

KNOLLE JERSEY FARMS OFFICE

KNOLLE JERSEY FARMS HEADQUARTERS
Barn No. 2

Visitors are always welcome.
Please telephone in advance
for reservations or tours for
large groups.

10 MILES TO SAN PATRICIO

139

Introduction

The days were sunny and the fields were bright. The magical growth of Knolle Jersey Farms and my own magical growth from childhood to adulthood coincided. Growing up on Knolle Jersey Farms in the 1940s and 50's, I experienced bountifulness. Smells of freshly cut silage. Waves of bluebonnets. Freezers full of the latest flavor of Knolle ice cream. Local newspapers featuring our prize-winning cattle. After a rain, we'd drive around to see creeks and ditches overflowing with water.

However, with the brimming fields came concern about the next drought. The jokes and stories that enlivened the conversation between the Knolle brothers and their employees were tempered by grueling work. They'd say, "No one milks cows for the fun of it."

In this book are many who aren't named but who also shaped Knolle Jersey Farms. My own view was limited, and it's impossible for me to list them all. With the help of my cousins, Pearson Knolle and A.W. Knolle, and a few key people like Arthur Jones Jr., this list emerged.

Nine milking barns had to be managed. Paul and Sonny Crisp were both overall managers. Among the individual barn managers were Lee Crisp, Sylvester Coffin, J.R. Gallimore, Armando Gonzales, Lucio Perez, Sr., Eduardo Gamez, Lupe DeLeon, Ricardo Leal, Heber Smith, and Ruben Cantu.

Cattle were milked at 2:00 am and 2:00 pm. Electricity had to be maintained at dairy barns and water wells at 15 locations over 15,000 acres (Pedro Olivarez, Juan Soto, and Joe Melig). Juan Cornejo, Jr. was one of the drivers who hauled the fresh milk into Corpus,

Feed crops were planted and harvested: and old tractors had to be continually repaired (Grady Crisp, Simon Garza, Lonzo Stewart). Tractor drivers such as

Clyde Oliver, Willis Oliver, D. C. Crisp, Bugs Crisp and Felipe Perez worked nonstop.

Baby calves were taken from their mothers early so the cows could go back into the milk barns. Calves were raised separately and required special attention. Arthur Jones was the overseer for the baby calves. Arthur Jones, Jr, Oliver Jones, Elmer Cox, Juan Rios, and Julian Rios were among those who took care of them.

Working at the Feed Barn, mixing feed according to specific formulas and hauling it to the cattle, were Lester Peterson, Rosebud Peterson, Lt. Eichenburger, John Earl Oliver, Lamar Peterson, Tom Edmonds. Charles Taylor, Riddley Rich, Tommy Bray, Vernon Rogers, Smith Walker, Willis Oliver, Willie Hill, Lester Allen, Albert Lopez, Sr., Horatio Lopez, Marcus Gonzales, Louis Roberts, Joe Hill, Ernest Rogers, and Johnny Lee Edmonds. Cattle going to state and national fairs were groomed, transported, and shown in the ring by Robert Weathers, Pancho Garza, and Reginald Buesnel. They traveled with the show cattle, hauling them in trucks and sometimes by rail.

Fences and homes had to be continually repaired (James Pearson, Max Almendarez, Mauro Perez).

Cowboys moved cattle on horseback over many miles (Juan Cornejo and Pete Vasquez) T.J. Garrett hauled cattle.

Others who come to mind are Tomas Olivarez, Geronimo Perez, Abelino Perez, Ramon Castro, Pedro Trevino, Roque Garza, Arturo Cavasos, Abel Cavasos, Lupe Trevino, George McCoy, Raul Olivarez, Jesus Olivarez, Jose Luis Olivarez, Carlos Olivarez, Miguel Ruiz, Alandro Ruiz, and Jesus de los Santos.

Skilled technicians were required for veterinary work, lab work, and artificial insemination (Ron Buesnel, Juan Alanis, Robert Alanis, Ruben Alanis, and Wayne Buesnel).

There were office workers who greeted visitors and kept financial records (Belle Gallagher, Candelario Leal, and Camilla Crisp). Some recorded milk weights, cattle registrations and health records (Minerva Chapa, Henrietta Zuniga, and Evangelina Alanis).

Some in charge of the Knolle Store over a period of 50 years were August Sturm, Antonio Salazar, C. W. West, Victor Schacrl, Don Lynch, and Margie Leal, Mary Perez, and Olivia Perez.

Scores of workers spent years on the Farm, chopping huisache and digging ditches in the South Texas sun. I've failed to list many names.

This section is about the growth of Knolle Jersey Farms narrated from my perspective as a maturing individual. The italicized sentences underneath the title of each story reflect the age of the narrator. Each narrator is a part of me.

All the States

It's 1951. I'm 9. I'm glad I live in the United States. It's the best country in the world. And Texas is the best state in the best country. And Sandia is the best town in Texas. And our farm is the best part of Sandia. I'm a lucky girl.

Mr. Harry Strohmeyer and I are sitting on the rug in front of our fireplace. We're working on a puzzle of the United States. We've already put nine wooden states on the board.

"Louise, do you know how many of these states I've traveled to?"

I shake my head. I'm trying to figure out where Montana goes.

"All 48."

I look up. "All the states? How'd you do that?"

"I go to farms and cattle shows everywhere to take pictures of cows. My pictures are in all the farm magazines. When I visit a dairy, everything stops but the milking. Everybody helps get the cows ready for me."

He takes Montana and puts it under Canada.

"I like for their horns and hoofs to be polished, and their tails brushed. Their front feet must be straight and opposite each other, and their rear feet must be spread apart to show off their udders. For the picture, I stand a little to the rear of the cows. They look better that way."

I already know what Mr. Strohmeyer is telling me. My daddy's taken me with him to watch. He always tells me to be still and quiet. The picture is supposed to show the cow looking alert. A man will stand behind Mr. Strohmeyer and holler. He'll wave a white sheet to make the cow look at him. The cow has to be just right. She has to have her head up and turned toward the camera. Mr. Strohmeyer will only snap the camera once.

Mr. Strohmeyer has a bad temper, and he'll get mad and say bad words. Yesterday, the workers tried and tried to get a cow's head in the right position. They'd holler and wave the sheet. Every time, the cow would look away. Mr. Strohmeyer exploded and threw his hat down. "That cow is cross-eyed. Take her away." He was right. She was cross-eyed. It didn't matter that she was beautiful.

Fig. 55 Harry Strohmeyer, Knolle Jersey Farms, circa 1960

Mr. Strohmeyer stays a week at our house, and Mama cooks big meals. We eat supper in the dining room. Mama and Mr. Strohmeyer stay up late and talk about New York and the opera. I like to listen, but I have to go to bed early. I get in bed and imagine going to all the states.

How to See a Horse in the Dark

It's 1953. I'm 11. I love my daddy. I'm only a girl, but I want to be just like my daddy. He's about perfect. I think about how smart he is, how kind and gentle he is. He loves me, and he loves our Farm.

"Daddy! The horses are gone! Dancer and Lucky Boy have run off."

My job is to feed our two horses before dark, I'd been watching "Captain Video" on our television. Now it's almost night, and they aren't up at the shed, and I can't find them anywhere. I feel terrible. I've lost our good horses.

"Don't worry, Weegee, it's okay. We'll find them. Let's have a look."

I follow Daddy. He's walking slowly. He's just come in from checking the milking. Tomorrow, he'll have to get up when it's still dark and go check everything all over again. After that, he'll meet with my uncles at the office. Then he goes to the shop to get the tractor drivers started. He always comes home in time to squeeze oranges and bring juice to me and Charles. He wants us to be at school on time.

I know he's tired, but Daddy's the only one who can help me. We go out to the backyard fence where the shed is. The shed's where we keep the trough and the feed. The fence is made of rough cedar posts, and I can climb through the railings. It's just tall enough to keep the cows out of the yard. I remember when Mama had thought the shed was ugly, so she'd had it painted dark green to go with the trees and the grass.

"Weegee, do you know how to find a horse in the dark?" I just shake my head. "Here, get down lower, and I'll show you."

Daddy gets down on the grass and looks through

the fence toward the pasture. I copy him. He points toward the horizon.

"There they are, do you see 'em?" I can. Dancer and Lucky Boy are right there against the sky.

"It's called skylining," he says quietly. "If you get down low, you can see animals, even at night."

We stay there for a while. The sky's getting darker. Daddy gives me a pat and goes back to the house and the new television.

"Here, Dancer. Here, Lucky Boy."

Poor Sheila

It's 1954, and I'm 12. I wear my hair in a ponytail and have some pretty clothes. I have a black velvet dress.

Sheila's breath is hot and wet and sour. I'm trying to lead her, and she's being even more stubborn than usual. I've been trying to get her to go in one direction, and my shoulders hurt.

Daddy always says, "Just practice with her every day after school, and she'll get easier to lead."

*Fig. 56 Louise, 12 yrs., with Sheila
in her backyard Sandia, Texas, 1954*

I've been practicing with Sheila every day getting her ready for the San Antonio Livestock Exhibition. Sheila has a good pedigree. Her full name is Masterman Monarch Sheila. She's a daughter of Masterman Standard Monarch, who is a son of Jester Aim, one of the two Century Sires owned by our farm. Sheila is also descended from our other Century Sire, Masterman Golden Jolly. He's the most famous Jersey bull ever.

Sheila should be easy to train. But she has a mind of her own and goes where she wants to. A month ago, in the show ring at our county fair, she charged the judges' stand with me hanging on and trying to pull her back.

Daddy gave Sheila to me, and he gave a calf named Eldora to Charles. Sheila and Eldora were little calves then, and they looked just alike. But now, everyone knows about Eldora. She has an almost perfect udder, and she's already won Grand Champion at the Jim Wells County Fair. Eldora knows just how to act in the show ring. She follows Charles' lead perfectly, and when they pause, she turns her head toward the judges. Charles doesn't even have to work with her.

Sheila and I are almost done practicing. The rumble of the cattle truck surprises me. I hadn't expected they'd be taking the cattle to San Antonio so soon. I'm glad I've brushed her so much, and I'm feeling good. We're ready.

Fig. 57 Charles, 10 yrs.
With cattle truck, 1954

Daddy's coming over to us. "Louise, we don't have room for Sheila in the truck. Maybe she can go next year. We need room for the cows we think will win. Don't worry. We'll all have a good time at the fair anyway."

I feel like crying. Sheila and I have worked so hard. I swallow and my eyes water, but Daddy can't tell how bad I feel.

Charles and Eldora win Grand Champion. I smile and try to be happy for them. Charles is quiet as usual, not all that excited. Daddy's quiet too, but I can see from his face he's happy enough for all of us.

Charles and Eldora get their picture on the front page of the *San Antonio Express*.

The Chance of a Lifetime, Every Year

It's 1956. I'm 14. What would you do if you were a girl surrounded by 4000 boys? This happens to me and Kathy and Carolyn every April when Boy Scouts from all over the Gulf Coast spend a weekend at our River Park.

Kathy and I are having our usual after-school talk on our party line.

"Kathy, next weekend the Boy Scouts will be down at the River. I'll let Carolyn know. What do you think we should wear?" We decide to check with Carolyn.

My father is Ed Knolle, and he's in charge of getting everything ready for the Boy Scout Camporee. Daddy's moving all the hands over to the River Park, except the milkers. Some of the men are clearing roads and making spaces for all the tents. The rest are clearing a big circle for the bonfire and stacking wood in the middle. They've already cleared parking areas for the buses and cars. There'll also be a water truck, a flatbed trailer with a speaker system, a first-aid station, and a truck with four thousand cartons of milk.

The River Park is part of Knolle Jersey Farms. It's full of old oak trees good for climbing, and we cousins like to grab for the moss when we can get high enough. I know the scouts will want to explore the steep banks and swim in the river like we do. But they aren't allowed to. The leaders keep them busy with contests like which team is the fastest at lighting a fire with only two pieces of flint.

At last, it's Friday morning, and from my bedroom window, I can see the road filled with buses and cars taking scouts to the Camporee. Daddy and I join the stream of cars, and we finally get to the dark green cabin they use for the Camporee headquarters. My uncle Henry's already there. Daddy introduces me to the head scout leader who smiles at me and turns to Daddy.

"Ed, I was just telling Henry we sure appreciate getting to come out here again."

"Glad to have you, Ben. Louise here has been looking forward to seeing all these boys."

They laugh. I want to get back to the car and go home. Daddy's sometimes very insensitive.

The next morning, Kathy and Carolyn come over to my house with their mothers. We want to get ready together. I'm glad Carolyn's going because she's the prettiest, and she's sure to attract the boys' attention. Kathy's pretty too, but mainly she's clever and will have good ideas about what we should do. I'm the most practical. I'm the organizer.

Our mothers are drinking coffee in the kitchen and laughing. Kathy, Carolyn, and I in my room, and we're comparing outfits. We're wearing dresses this year. Kathy's hanging her dress in my closet and laughs.

"What if it's windy? We'll have to spend the whole time holding our skirts down."

"Oh no!" Carolyn jumped up. "I forgot about the wind."

I try to calm her. "Don't worry, Carolyn. We haven't had a strong wind in weeks. It doesn't blow that much at the river anyway."

Our mothers' laughter is now at the front porch, and from my window, I see my aunts Dorothy and Grace driving off. Kathy suggests playing records, and we stretch out on the carpet. We listen to "Love me Tender" and "Wake up Little Susie." A few weeks before, Kathy and I'd seen a really good movie called *The Student Prince*, and we'd both gotten the album. We play it for Carolyn.

After a while, Mother comes in.

"Maybe you girls should start getting ready. Ed wants to take you down there about 2:00." We scream and rush to the closet and grab our petticoats, dresses, and shoes. Carolyn screams again.

"What's wrong?" I fear the worst. Maybe she's hurt.

"I forgot my slip. Now the boys will be able to see through my dress."

I try to make it okay. "Carolyn, put everything on and look in the mirror. I don't think there's any way the scouts can see through all those petticoats."

Kathy sits at the end of the bed and rolls her eyes. "I don't know, Carolyn, with all that wind and no slip…"

Carolyn wails, "I can't go."

"Yoo-hoo." Carolyn's mother, Grace, walks in the front door and comes down the hall.

"Carolyn, I found this slip in your room. I thought you might need it.

"Oh, Mama, thank you so much. I definitely need it."

Kathy turns toward Grace. "All of us need it," she says, and everyone laughs, even Carolyn.

Mother comes in. "Ed's here, and he's in a hurry. Are you girls about ready?"

Fig. 58 Gulf Coast Boy Scout Camporee, 1956

Off we go. Daddy drives us down the winding road to the River. Our first sight of the Camporee is hundreds of tents lined up in sections with flags for each troop. Boys in dark green uniforms are swarming around.

Kathy leans closer to the car window. "It's like a little town."

Carolyn and I have been hoping that Kathy will come up with some kind of plan. But the rest of the afternoon is boring. Over and over, we walk along the paths between the tents. The boys are all too busy making fires and having knottying contests to notice us. We even walk over to the First Aid Station to see if anyone's gotten hurt. Carolyn gets whistled at one time. That just makes Kathy and me feel worse.

Fig. 59 Camporee Campfire, 1956

We go back on Saturday night with our parents to the bonfire. Daddy and Henry make welcoming speeches, and the three other Knolle brothers are introduced. The leaders and parents thank the Knolles for their hospitality.

The Boy Scouts sing campfire songs like "Oh My Darling Clementine" and "You are my Sunshine." We all laugh and holler. Then it's over. We're leaving, and our cousin Ginny runs up.

"I bet you had a great time today! Do you think I can go next year?"

"Sure Ginny." Carolyn smiles at her. Kathy grins, "You'll be old enough next year. It was a blast, Ginny."

And we all agree. We can't wait till next year. After all, it's the chance of a lifetime.

Tractors and Toilet Paper

It's 1962. I'm 20. I'd taken a year out of college to travel as American Dairy Princess. I'm eager to get back to SMU and my boyfriend, Roger, and my best friend, Carmen.

It was a late August evening. I loved those days on our farm when it was beginning to cool off a bit, and rain clouds were on the horizon. My father, Ed and I were standing on the highest point of a pasture behind the dairy barn he'd given Charles and me. We were standing next to a new water well, and he was explaining his idea for irrigating the pasture.

"You see, Weegee, the water will flow down the hill between the rows of dirt."

I could see what he was talking about. Rows of overturned dirt about 10 yards apart went down the slope from the top of the hill. Ruben must have just made them. I could smell the fresh-turned soil.

The water well was at the highest point in the pasture, but all there was to see was a pipe. Everything else was underground. The submersible pump was down at the water level, and it would push the water to the surface. The water would then flow down between all the rows.

"Now, Weegee, we'll use this surveying scope to mark lines going all around the hill and crossing the rows. Each line has to be at an exact right angle to the rows and at the same level going all the way around."

I nodded.

"Okay, now go down the slope part way, and I'll show you where to put the toilet paper to mark where the lines need to go. If the wind starts blowing, just bury the end of each piece a little way into the dirt. Ruben will follow the pieces of toilet paper with the tractor and mound up the soil to make the lines. The lines will slow the water long enough to fill up the sections before it spills over into the next level. This way, the water will slowly cover the whole pasture."

Fig. 60 Water flowing from the submersible pump, Knolle Jersey Farms, 1962

While I was listening to my father, I was torn. I was excited about leaving soon to go back to SMU. But our farm always pulled me back. And now, he was showing me his new idea for a way to irrigate our land. He wanted me to understand what he was doing for the land he'd just given Charles and me. He'd be drilling shallow wells at the highest points in the pastures and using small pumps to get the water to the surface. Then, gravity would take over and send the water down the slopes. The rows and lines divided the land into sections and slowed the water as it went, and more of it would be absorbed by the soil. No need for powerful and expensive pumps lifting huge volumes of water from deep wells.

And so, with the surveying tools and a roll of toilet paper, we started running lines across the slope for Ruben to follow with our John Deere 420. Ed would look through the scope and use hand motions to signal where I should go. Sometimes, I'd be close enough to hear him say, "You're too low. Come forward." Or he would direct me, "Keep going that way. Okay, that's good. Mark it." I followed his directions and put pieces of white toilet paper in the dirt for Ruben to see from the tractor.

Growing up on the Farm, I'd known that the generally accepted opinion in South Texas was that we didn't have enough water to irrigate. "This isn't West Texas, you know," they'd say. "There, farmers have deep wells that reach down to plenty of water underground."

But we needed water. The drought of the 50's had been devastating to South Texas and the Farm. We'd had to cut down our mesquite trees, so the cattle could feed on the beans. By the end of that decade, landowners were no longer permitted to pump water out of the Nueces River. Ed knew we didn't have enough underground water for the typical West Texas deep well, but he knew his land. This was pastureland, and he knew the Coastal Bermuda grass didn't require large amounts of water. His plan was to drill numerous shallow wells and irrigate only when we were threatened with drought.

"I think this will work, Weegee. If it does, I'll put wells all over the Farm."

And so, when I came back from SMU the following summer, his project was in full swing. I became his ready assistant with the ever-present toilet paper roll and the surveying tools. I could tell Ed was glad to have me back. Almost every day he'd asked me if I would help him. Everyone else complained that the job of following Ed's orders with the toilet paper was hot and boring. It was.

*Fig. 61 Lines of overturned dirt creating an even flow of water,
part of Knolle Jersey Farms' irrigation system, 1962*

In the year I'd been gone, he'd learned a lot. During that year, he'd drilled several wells throughout the Farm. His first step was to put the well in the right place. The well had to be above everything he wanted to irrigate. Ed had also realized it was best not to place the well on top of a steep hill, or the water would run down too quickly and not have time to soak in.

"Never let the water go into the ditch by the road," he'd say.

That second summer, I'd begun to understand that Ed was the only one who could see the big picture. "Weegee, one or two men with shovels will be able to irrigate hundreds of acres just by repairing the rows where the water breaks through. Soon we'll have wells all over the Farm."

The Princess and the Bull and Other Tales

It's 1963. I'm 21. Last year I was American Dairy Princess and traveled to 48 states and South America. I'm glad to be back at SMU.

"Louise, you know better than that. After all I've taught you about cattle! You could've been killed!"

Fig. 62 American Dairy Princess Louise Knolle with Sparkling Success Basil, Oct. 14, 1961, photo scanned from the Columbus Dispatch.

I was 20 at the time, and my job for that year had been to travel across the country as American Dairy Princess. My father, Ed, had seen a picture of me at the cattle show in Columbus, Ohio. It was a close-up of me holding a Grand Champion Jersey Bull with my face next to the bull's head.

"But Daddy, the photographer asked me to pose that way."

You should have said 'no', Weegee. You know more about cattle than any news photographer. That bull could've turned on you in an instant, and your face was right there next to his horns."

Jersey bulls are among the most hostile and dangerous of all cattle breeds. And I've always known never to go into a pasture with a Jersey bull in it. A Jersey bull will run across the field and attack for no reason at all. One of our prize-winning bulls Ambassador is so aggressive that he's got be given a shot of a tranquilizer every time he goes into the show ring. A bull's behavior is an inherited trait, and most of Ambassador's daughters are as unpredictable as he is. Daddy says a cow that breaks through a fence is usually a daughter of Ambassador.

Our mature breeding bulls are kept in separate pens next to the main milking barn near the office. Each pen is double fenced. Daddy has a scar on his hand caused by a bull. He was in one of the bull pens when a bull got after him. He jumped over the fence but left his hand on the fence rail a bit too long. The bull hit the fence rail, and his horn cut a deep gash in Daddy's hand.

One bull had killed a man. Manuel Garza lived next to Dairy Barn #3. Manuel helped take care of the milk cows there, and he'd raised a little Jersey bull as a pet in the backyard of his house. Daddy had warned him of the danger of keeping the bull too long, but Manuel hung on to his pet. The calf grew into a young bull.

One night, about 2:00 am, Manuel went out to the pasture to get the cows up for milking. The cows were gentle and came easily into the milk barn. Manuel located the milk cows in the pasture and was guiding them into the holding pen next to the barn. He wasn't aware that his pet bull had gotten out of the backyard and had joined the herd of milk cows. It was a dark night, and there was no way Manuel could have seen him. The bull attacked Manuel and gored him to death.

Lots of other things can go wrong on a dairy farm. In the summertime, the most important job is putting up cattle feed for the next year. Grain crops like milo and corn are harvested and stored in trench silos. Each trench silo is a ditch, 120 feet long and 30 feet deep.

Fig. 63 Caterpillar tractor packing down silage
Knolle Jersey Farms, 1963

Dump trucks haul the feed down into the trench silos, and tractors come along behind to pack it down. The feed ferments underground and is used the following year.

On a hot summer day, the fumes caused by the fermentation process can be deadly.

One afternoon, Ed went by one of the silos to see how much feed had been put up that day. He found all eight of the workers standing frozen on the edge of the silo, looking down into it. Around 20 feet down at the bottom was Alfredo Perez, lying there unconscious. Three dead rabbits were beside him. Ed took off his shirt, wrapped it around his mouth and nose, went down into the silo, and pulled Alfredo out.

When I asked my cousin A.W. about the silo story, he laughed and told me a second part. A.W. had been at the shop early one morning and had heard Ed fuming about Alfredo missing work again. He hadn't turned up for several days.

Ed slammed the hood of the pick-up. "Durn that Alfredo, I should've left him down there."

The Office

It's 1968. I'm 26. Butch and I are living in San Antonio and planning to move back to the farm. We want to build a house and raise a family there. I drive to Sandia every week to work in the office for a few days.

The annual meeting of the Texas and Southwestern Cattle Raisers Association draws a big crowd for its lecture sessions and parties. Butch and I were at the closing fiesta on the San Antonio River Walk. I ran into Julia Jitkoff, the daughter of my father's good friend, John Armstrong.

"So, what do you do on your ranch, Louise?"

I'd always been a bit intimidated by Julia and wished I could say I did the branding or rounded up cattle on horseback.

"Well, I spend most of my time in our office doing the bookkeeping."

"Of course," Julia said with a gleam in her eye. "I do that too. That's where the power is, you know."

I smiled at this sudden revelation about myself. Maybe I was doing the bookkeeping because I wanted to be in the center of things. My father, Ed, wasn't interested in the books, but I knew how critical they were. I learned where the money was going, I knew everything that was happening on the entire Farm, and no one was telling me what to do. It was a good job for a girl who wanted an important place.

I'm 26 now, but I've never forgotten the little 10-year-old who just wanted a job. My first job had been to sit in the office during the noon hour and answer the phone. The office was silent then, though it might have been full of people and emergencies just the hour before. I've never told anyone how frightened I was. I'd sit alone at the big desk and face the phone. I was terrified it might ring.

I made 50 cents an hour, which amounted to 50 cents a day. It was good pay at the time, but the Knolle Store was about 10 yards from the back door of the office, and the Store had a complete selection of Knolle Ice Cream Products. I usually settled on an extra-large Dixie cup of vanilla ice cream with chocolate swirls. I felt less afraid at the desk eating the ice cream, and I got into the habit of buying ice cream for lunch every day. I'd wanted to make money that summer, but I soon realized I was spending my entire salary on ice cream. I kept buying it anyway.

Fig. 64 Knolle Jersey Farms Store, 1944

The next summer I'd gotten longer hours and was actually helpful. Mrs. Gallagher taught me how to record show winnings and production records in the black books. Sometimes, she'd let me work on cattle pedigrees, and I began to teach myself to type and use the adding machine.

Mrs. Gallagher ran the office and had been there since the beginning. Everyone called her Belle. I still call her Mrs. Gallagher because she was my first boss. She kept all the records and pedigrees, and she wrote letters and checks and kept track of everything. When Mrs. Gallagher paid the electricity bill, she would tuck her own personal check into the Farms' envelope to save herself the three-cent stamp.

The old Farm office was a wooden building, shotgun style, filled with dark, wooden desks and metal file cabinets. It was always dusty. Mrs. Gallagher's area shared the front space with a meeting room. Walton's work area was in the back near the door that led directly outside to the Store. Near Walton's desk on a shelf was a glass jar filled with formaldehyde and the fetus of a two-headed calf.

Fig. 65 Bob and Henry Knolle office front porch, 1944

The office front porch was where the five Knolle brothers met at 5:30 in the morning, seven days a week, to organize the day. Henry was the oldest one. He was a driving force in the Farms' growth, purchasing land and instinctively knowing the ins and outs of cattle breeding. He made sure the Knolle name was known and that the Farms was recognized early as a leader in the world of Jersey cattle.

The second Knolle brother, Arthur, had had his own flying school in Alice during the war years, but in 1948 he joined Knolle Jersey Farms to pursue his other love: farming.

Fig. 66 Arthur's Flying Service and School, Alice, Texas, 1944

Arthur took charge of growing corn, red top cane, hegari, and various sorghums on 2000 acres of farmland to provide feed for the cattle. Arthur and Ed devised a system of canals for sprinkler irrigation, and later they planted thousands of acres of drought tolerant Coastal Bermuda grass.

The third brother, Bob, operated the feed mill that turned out 10 tons of mixed feed every day. Bob was good with people, and thirty men worked for him in the feed barn. They mixed the grain according to specific formulas and loaded it into trucks for distribution to the dairy cattle, the bulls, the baby calves, the heifers, and the dry cows.

Ed was the fourth Knolle brother, and early on, in 1931, he'd partnered with Henry and their father, Almond. Eventually their first 12 grade Jersey cows became a herd of 8000 Jersey cattle, and Ed became the general manager of Knolle Jersey Farms. On a day-to-day basis, he organized and supervised the milking, the breeding, the farm hands, and the fieldwork.

Walton was the youngest of the brothers and the most organized of the five. He kept records on the 1600 calves that were raised every year on the Farm. Each calf had to be registered with the American Jersey Cattle Club. Each had a registration number, a registration certificate, and an official name based on its pedigree. Each had a tattoo for Farm identification and health records of their vaccinations and health history.

Fig. 67 Walton and Ed, Knolle Jersey Farms office, 1944

Looking back at my time in the old office, I remember how much fun it was. One Knolle family trait is a good sense of humor, and practical jokes abounded. It was not unusual for Mrs. Gallagher to find a rubber snake or a plastic bug in her desk. Ed would hold one of his photographs up-side-down and tell an unassuming worker that the picture was made with an upside-down camera. Walton had put a speaker on his car radio, and whenever Robert Weathers walked by, Walton would turn it on, and Robert would think an unseen person was talking to him.

But the Farm outgrew the old office, and in 1959, it was replaced by a sprawling red brick building, ranch style. In the visitors' room, there's a trophy cabinet, a display case for show ribbons and banners, and a freestanding bulletin board for the latest pictures and newspaper clippings. Wide glass windows look out over the Farm and the few cars on the road. There are spacious offices for Ed and Henry, two large work areas, a separate payroll area, and a tiled laboratory for milk testing and veterinary work. The modern restrooms have a ladies' lounge area with a dresser and sofa.

The Farm has always been so big and spread out that it's hard to communicate with everyone working there. For the new office, Ed devised a strip of colored light bulbs to place in the front window. Each manager has his own color: green for Ed, yellow for Paul, red for Grady, blue for Sonny. When the bulb is twisted, the color lights up. All the managers know to check for their color when they drive by. It saves a lot of time and trouble.

By 1959 my uncles didn't come by much anymore. Henry is now in charge of the milk plant in Corpus. Arthur, Bob, and Walton all have their own farms. The new office is staffed by two long-time employees, Candelario Leal and Camilla Crisp, who handle the bookkeeping and secretarial work. My good friends, Minerva, Keta, and Evangeline record milk weights and health records.

A few years after the new office was built, Mrs. Gallagher retired. She and I spent weeks going over all the land abstracts, surveys, field notes, legal records. She taught me how and when each tract of land was purchased and all its pertinent information such as percentages of ownership and mineral rights. I'm now one of the few who knows how things came to be.

Fig. 68 Camilla Crisp and Belle Gallagher
Belle's retirement party
Knolle Jersey Farms, 1962

I like my responsible role in the new office, but I keep looking back to the old office and the hours I spent under Mrs. Gallagher's guidance. Was it the first time I felt needed? Is it nostalgia? I don't know.

I do know that my heart is still in that old office, its three dusty and crowded rooms that gave me a chance to be feel grown up.

What's in a Name?

It's 1972. I'm 30. When Hurricane Celia hit the Farm in 1970, Butch and I were still living in San Antonio. Our plans to move to the farm were interrupted by Celia. A lot has changed since then.

Butch and I were having dinner at La Fonda with our friends Barbie and Rick, and we'd been talking about the storm in the Gulf. I became restless and went to the pay phone to call home.

"Daddy, are you worried about the hurricane?"

"Hi Weegee...Not really. They say it's going to come in north of Corpus. I'm just hoping we get a little rain out of it." I was relieved, and after talking a few minutes, we hung up.

The next afternoon, Celia abruptly changed course, and 125 mph winds hit Corpus bringing very little rain and no storm surge. Tornados were spawned inland, and wind gusts measuring 150 mph damaged the Farm.

After Celia hit Knolle Jersey Farms, roads had to be cleared, 100 miles of fencing had to be rebuilt, milking barns repaired, and windows, roofs, and walls had to be replaced for over 80 tenant houses. The new Knolle Jersey Farms office building had stood firm during the storm, and it had been a place of refuge for many of the people living on the Farm.

The oak trees at the River Park were so torn up that, after 25 years, the Knolle brothers never had another Boy Scout Camporee.

Cattle survive natural disaster better than we do; the only cattle hurt were those hit by flying objects. But milk production was never again as high as it had been the day before the storm. Without power and with only two small generators, it was impossible to get 4500 cows milked twice a day. After a week, the cows began to dry up. By the time the Jerseys returned to normal milk production, my father Ed and his brother, Henry, had dissolved their partnership of 45 years.

A year after Celia, in 1971, Ed, and Henry sold the milk processing plant, Knolle Jersey Milk Products, to Hygeia Dairy Company, and after that, they began dissolving the assets they owned together.

Butch and I moved to the Farm in 1971. One day, I stopped by my parents' house to see them. They were sitting at the kitchen table having lunch and talking about Ed and Henry's plans to dissolve their partnership.

"Ed, the name Knolle Jersey Farms is the most important thing. You've been a quiet and steady partner, and, if you don't get the name, no one will know you've even been here."

To my mother, Mary Margaret, the name Knolle Jersey Farms was more important than the land her husband and his brother were partitioning. I knew she'd watched my father working long days for almost 40 years, hardly ever leaving his careful oversight of the Farms' operation. She wanted him to be recognized for his role in the family enterprise.

In a way, she was right. Ed and Henry had both received rewards and recognition for their accomplishments, but Henry was the friendly, gregarious one and had always been the public face of Knolle Jersey Farms. In 1954, Henry and his family had moved Corpus, so Henry could devote full time to managing the processing plant that supplied milk products to the Coastal Bend region of South Texas.

Ed had quietly managed the day-to-day business of Knolle Jersey Farms. He made sure the milking went smoothly at each of the nine barns and that the field work, planting and harvesting 4000 acres of feed, progressed with no serious trouble. He had supervised the breeding, the feeding, the milking and the employees.

The other three Knolle brothers, Walton, Bob, and Arthur had joined the family business later and had each made important contributions, Walton with the young cattle, Bob with the feeding operation, and Arthur with the farming and grass planting.

Friends and acquaintances often expressed amazement that there'd never been any serious rivalry between the brothers and that they'd managed to work so well together for so long. Every morning around 6:00, they met at the steps of the Farm Office to plan their day and to share jokes and football stories. The brothers helped each other and depended on each other, a tradition begun and encouraged by their father, Almond Knolle.

Almond had begun searching for land to buy "for his son" when his first son Henry was born in 1906. Family stories say that Almond used Aesop's fable of a bundle of sticks to teach his eight children that they would be stronger when they could work together. They had followed his advice then, and Henry and Ed followed his example when it came time to partition their land. They had seen their father partition his land in the 1950s.

In their early years together Almond, Henry, and Ed had amassed 10,000 acres of land. In the 1950s when he was over 70, Almond had given up his partnership in Knolle Jersey Farms and divided his portion of the land evenly among his five sons and his three daughters, Mary, Katherine, and Ruth.

Now Ed and Henry as the two remaining partners had decided to dissolve Knolle Jersey Farms. They were in their 60's, their children were grown, and the processing plant had been sold. It was time to divide the land. They didn't need an expensive appraisal of the property. No one knew the land as well as they. Their plan was simple. One of them would divide the land, and the other would get to choose first. The plan worked.

Only one decision remained. Which brother would

retain the name Knolle Jersey Farms? They decided to use a simple bidding process. It turned out that Ed was wiling to pay more for the name than Henry.

Ed and Henry honored their mutual decisions.

The Knolle brothers continued to meet at daybreak for as long as they lived.

The Damn Dam

It's 1976. I'm 34. After the dam issue was settled in 1974, I had several opportunities to go into politics, but I wanted to stay on my farm and have babies. I guess I wasn't really interested in politics because it never occurred to me I could do both.

"We've got to do something about the R&M dam situation. If we don't stop this, nobody else is going to."

My mother, Mary Margaret, was always pushing us to do something about something, and she was usually right.

She was right this time. A Houston billionaire oilman Oscar Wyatt was using his money and political influence to persuade people in Corpus Christi to support the R&M dam site near Calallen. The alternative site being considered was Choke Canyon near Three Rivers. Wyatt had conducted an unofficial opinion poll in Corpus to determine how people felt about the Calallen dam site. A few days before the poll, Oscar Wyatt had held a big rally with free tamales to get out the vote for the R&M dam site. In the poll, R&M had won over Choke Canyon by a wide margin of 32,000 votes. Oscar Wyatt considered Corpus Christi his home base, but no one could figure out why the R&M dam site was so important to him.

It was easy to figure out that Corpus needed an additional water supply to accommodate its increasing population and its growing industry. It was also easy to figure out that the R&M dam site would result in a larger lake to supply more water. It was easy to see that a larger lake would have a higher value for real estate and industrial developers. It was also easy to see that a larger lake would be the costlier choice.

Not only would R&M be more costly in dollars,

but it would come at great human cost as well. The R&M site would flood a more highly populated area and destroy communities and livelihoods. The site would also destroy the agricultural production of a fertile area, long recognized for its high yield.

The R&M site would be costly as well to the historical legacy of South Texas. In San Patricio, early cemeteries, landmarks, and historic homes would be inundated.

Lost as well would be a precarious ecological balance. The R&M dam would prevent fresh river water from flowing into the estuaries and bays. In Corpus, environmental leaders Hans Suter and Henry Hildebrand expressed concern about the impact the large R&M dam would have on the reproduction of fish and shellfish.

The dam proposed for the Choke Canyon site would be smaller and would be located at a natural choke site on the Frio River. The surrounding area was rocky with soil of mostly caliche, and ranching predominated. The two towns most affected, Three Rivers and Campbellton, were not unified in opinion.

But the Knolle family in Sandia was unified, and others with reasons of their own joined in the fight against the R&M dam site. For the Knolles, it was economic and personal. The R&M dam would heavily impact Knolle Jersey Farms and the people it employed. Knolle Jersey Farms had provided milk for Corpus Christi for over 40 years. At its height, the Farms had directly and indirectly employed 200-250 people. About half of all the land would be covered by the resulting lake which would be muddy and shallow because of the rich soil and the relatively flat terrain.

My mother and I got to work and organized the family to form a political group called South Texans for Choke Canyon. We decided it was better to be 'for' Choke Canyon than to be 'against' R&M. I was to be the chairman of the group. My married name, Schimmel, would be more politically acceptable than the name Knolle, so it had to be me.

I was at a desk in my parents' house, trying to figure out a way to get started with the new group. The phone rang, and it was my cousin Pearson trying to find me with some news.

"Louise, I've just heard about a meeting about the dam site. All the Coastal Bend County Commissioners are getting together next Wednesday. The commissioners from Corpus are already behind the R&M site, and they're planning to get the commissioners from the other counties to vote for it. They want to get them all unified for R&M."

"Oh Pearson, this might be our chance."

The next day, Pearson and I called each of the County Commissioners of the 12-county Coastal Bend area. The conversations went something like this:

"Hello, this is Louise Schimmel, chairman of South Texans for Choke Canyon. I'm calling to let you know how important your vote will be at the County Commissioners meeting next week. Will you be attending?"

"Well, I'm not sure. I guess I can go if it's that important."

"Good. It's really important that you be there. You know how Corpus tries to boss all of us small town people around. Now, they're trying to push this R&M dam through, and it'll benefit no one but them."

"Really? Well, we don't want them to push us around. You can count on my vote for sure."

On Wednesday, during the meeting, the R&M proposal got 11 votes from the Corpus Christi delegates. The Choke Canyon proposal got 13. Choke Canyon won all 12 of the area votes plus 1 from Corpus.

The next week we called the 12 County Commissioners.

I say, "Hello, I'm calling for South Texans for Choke Canyon. We'd like to thank you for your vote at the meeting last week. We're looking for a committee chairman from your county. And we know you're a county leader, and we'd like to ask you to take this position. All you'd have to do is circulate a petition in your county."

"Well, I guess I could do that. We sure don't want Corpus to run over us."

Since I was the chairperson of South Texans for Choke Canyon, I was interviewed by various Corpus television stations. I gave talks at service organizations like the Lions and Rotary Clubs, and I became easily recognizable by my long blond braid over one shoulder. Whenever I was asked about my special interest in being a landowner, I would say, "Yes, I'm a landowner, but I prefer the name 'landkeeper'. No one really owns the land. It's only in our keeping for the short time we're on this earth."

After about three weeks of circulating petitions, we'd gathered 32,000 signatures and stopped at that symbolic number. We had the petitions bound and copied to take to Austin for the hearing before the three Texas Water Rights commissioners. People from all over Texas showed up. I presented our signed petitions, 32,000 names, which made Oscar Wyatt's politicking ineffective. The Houston billionaire oilman stood up and spoke about our petitions in a condescending manner, but he could no longer say what 'the people' wanted.

The engineers then testified.

The commissioners chose Choke Canyon.

Fig. 69 The old Mathis Dam, circa 1940

Doing What He Had to Do

It's 1983, and I'm 41. Butch and I divorced last year, and I have purchased a small house in Corpus for me and the boys. It's too painful to go back to the Farm these days.

Milk is perishable. Keeping it clean and fresh was top priority on our Farm. The fresh milk had to be kept cool at all times, so the milk was stored in a cooling tank powered by a gasoline engine.

In the early years of the dairy farm, the Knolles had an old gasoline engine which was hard to keep running. If the engine broke, an entire tank of milk would be lost, so my father, Ed, slept on the ground every night next to that old engine. If it stopped running, the silence would wake him up, and he would fix it. Ed was a steady and silent man. He was good at keeping Knolle Jersey Farms going. His older brother, Henry, had an outgoing personality and the vision to propel them forward, but it seemed as if he just walked past the engine, it would break. They agreed that Henry would stay away from the milk cooler.

The fresh milk was placed in numbered milk cans and taken in the family's old truck to the Mistletoe Creamery in Corpus. In those days, the roads were unpaved and muddy, so the trips could take up to twelve hours, depending on how many things went wrong.

Ed likes to tell about the trip he made when he had five flats and two wrecks on what was called the "Five Mile Road." Now it's County Road 3088. He'd stop and borrow neighbors' trucks along the way, but the borrowed vehicle often had more problems than the one left behind. At one point after dark, Ed borrowed a truck, realized it didn't have any lights and soon ran into a carful of people who were in another vehicle without lights.

As the Farm grew, milk production increased, and transporting milk to Corpus Christi in individual milk cans became more and more difficult. The milk didn't remain at a constant temperature in the milk cans, and there was also the problem of the time and labor it took to unload the increasing number of cans. Most dairies remained small and were resigned to the use of milk cans for hauling milk.

In the mid-1930s, Ed devised a plan for their growing dairy business. He contacted the Heil Company in Milwaukee, Wisconsin and sent them his design for a milk truck with a thermos tank. The Heil Company was well known throughout the country for making all kinds of transport trucks, particularly milk trucks.

Fig. 70 The Heil Company, Milwaukee, Wisconsin
Ed Knolle at right
With the milk truck Ed designed, 1936.

They agreed to make a truck according to Ed's design, and in 1936, Ed and Mary Margaret flew to Milwaukee to pick up the truck. [See Appendix 4, page 263, for Mary Margaret's sketch made on the trip home in the new milk truck.] This was the first milk truck designed specifically to keep the milk at a constant temperature while being transported. After that, the Heil Company began selling the milk trucks, but they never gave Ed credit for the invention. Ed didn't care about getting credit. He'd done what he had to do.

Soon another situation arose. In the 1940s, the Knolle brothers began putting up ensilage to feed the Jerseys during the winter months. It was a long process. In the fields, tractor-drawn ensilage cutters would fill several trucks and trailers with chopped feed.

The trucks and trailers would drive to the side of deep trench silos where workers would shovel the feed into the silos below. Then bulldozers would move back and forth over the silage to pack it down.

This method of filling the trench silos was unsatisfactory to Ed because of the amount of time and labor that it took to shovel the chopped feed into the silos. So Ed took a gravel dump truck and enlarged it, so the feed could be dumped quickly instead of being shoveled.

Soon the Farm had a fleet of feed dump trucks. A big tractor would pull the feed dump truck down into the silo, and the truck would dump its load of feed before being pulled out again. Men would simply use shovels to spread the feed around in the silo. Problem solved.

Years later, Ed devised an irrigation system to use in times of drought. He created a system of shallow wells and gravity-flow irrigation to save labor and expensive equipment. The problem of water evaporation was also solved.

My father and I are driving away from the #9 dairy after we'd worked the cattle there.

"Daddy, what would you do if you didn't have all these cows?"

He looks back toward the barn and smiles.

"Grow flowers."

Meeting Mr. Cummins

It's 2004, and I'm 62. My father, Ed, is 92. The most important thing in my life now is that I'm commuting to the Episcopal Seminary of the Southwest in Austin. I'm hoping to get a master's degree. Last year, I was diagnosed with ALS, and I think being in seminary is keeping my focus away from myself. Ed doesn't understand why I want to go to seminary, and he'll never believe I have ALS. Nowadays, he likes to reminisce.

"Do you see that curb on the street corner?"

I nod my head. Of course, I see it. A.W. and I glance at each other and grin. Odem isn't that big, and the street curb is about the only thing there. A.W.'s taking Ed on his bi-monthly trip to pick up our cattle check, and I'm going along for the ride. We'll probably stop in Mathis to pick up barbecue.

Ed points toward the street corner and keeps talking. "That's where Henry and I sat, waiting with our money for Mr. Cummins. That's when we bought the last of the Taft Ranch cattle. It was 1940. Masterman Golden Jolly was in that group. He was nine years old."

In the 1930s and early 1940s, Ben Cummins had been the manager of the well-known Taft Ranch Jersey Herd. He'd purchased the cattle and then sold them to Henry and Ed. The Taft Ranch had been owned by Charles Phelps Taft, half-brother of President William Howard Taft.

"I didn't know Masterman Golden Jolly was nine when you got him. Was he already proven?" A.W. asks. He and Ed have always been close but especially now since A.W.'s father Walton has died and since Ed has lost his son Charles.

"Oh, no," Ed smiles. "The Taft Ranch had been

using him, but his daughters hadn't been tested or classified. They looked good to Henry and me though. We liked his daughters' uniformity and good udders. That's why we started using him as our herd sire."

I lean forward from the backseat.

"But he had a good pedigree too, didn't he, Daddy?"

"Of course, his grandsire and his dam were both from Jersey Island."

The year after purchasing Taft Ranch cattle, Ed and Henry had driven to Canada with their friend, Bob Almond, in hopes of purchasing another herd sire. They stopped at cattle shows and Jersey farms along the way, so it was a long trip. Ed wrote to Mary Margaret from Louisville, Kentucky:

Dear Mary Margaret,

Here we are in Kentucky. It seems good to be on the way home, but it will be several days yet as the National [Jersey Show] is Thurs. and Fri. I am writing with an old pen point stuck in the end of a pencil as I left my pen in the car.

We bought a bull in Canada and are very pleased with him. He cost $1500 and is about a year old. Bob [Almond] and Henry have gone to bed. ... I miss you very much and hate to be gone for so long. I'm bringing you a surprise from Canada, but it is not much. ...

Lots of love and goodnight, Ed

The $1500 bull they bought in Canada was Jester Aim. They bred him to the daughters of Masterman Golden Jolly, and Jester Aim proved to be the second

Fig. 71A Masterman Golden Jolly (1932-1948)

major herd sire of Knolle Jersey Farms.

In 1943, Knolle Jersey Farms had its first official classification, providing the Knolles a tool for advertising the physical appearance of their cattle. Official judges from the American Jersey Cattle Club classified 40 Jerseys, and 400 people were invited to a barbecue to observe the event. By 1951, 4027 registered Jerseys on the Farms had been classified. In a short time, Knolle Jersey Farms became internationally known.

Their achievement was made possible through the use of artificial insemination begun in the early 1940s, about the time they bought Jester Aim to breed to Masterman Golden Jolly's daughters. By 1951 over 50% of the Knolle herd had been bred artificially, and thousands of registered Jerseys had been tested and classified. They ranked in the top brackets of milk production and classification.

Masterman Golden Jolly became the most renowned animal ever to live on Knolle Jersey Farms. He sired more tested and classified daughters than any other sire of the Jersey breed, including many production champions and show ring winners.

In 1961, Masterman Golden Jolly and Jester Aim were two of the only five Jersey bulls chosen to be Century Sires, the American Jersey Cattle Club's highest designation. Ed and Henry Knolle became the only two brothers to be individually awarded the American Jersey Cattle Club's Master Breeder Award, Ed in 1961 and Henry in 1991.

The Farm's 50 years of success breeding Jersey cattle was still on my mind as A. W. turned the car toward Mathis. I glanced at my father. He was gazing out the window with a slight smile on his face. I could tell he was still on that street corner in Odem.

"Get Pete to Have a Look at It."

I'm 73. It's 2015. My father, Ed, died in 2010. I've grown up. John and I have been living on our farm for almost 20 years. It's home to both of us now.

John and I were sitting at our kitchen table with Ada and Duncan, our friends who'd come from Victoria to spend the night. They were almost ready to go home, but their car wouldn't start.

John said, "Get Pete to have a look at it. He can fix anything."

And sure enough, when Pete came along, he had the car running in minutes. Before any of us could even thank him, Pete went on his way. He liked to work quietly and all alone.

Pedro Olivarez had been employed by Knolle Jersey Farms for over 50 years. When he was 19, he'd volunteered to drive a load of cattle when no one else was around to do it, and so he'd become the cattle truck driver. Soon Ed realized Pete was good at fixing engines, and he was promoted to working in the maintenance shop. Eventually Pete was placed in charge of the electrical equipment at all nine dairies and became the person to call whenever there was trouble at one of the water wells. Pete became such a valuable employee that when Ed sold his dairy cattle and had to cut his workforce down to one person, he realized that Pete was the only person he couldn't do without.

One day in January, I remarked to Pete that I'd just had a birthday, and he said his was coming up the next month. We discovered that we were almost exactly the same age. So I got out my old Mathis school annual. I finally found a picture of Pete when he was nine.

He has on a white shirt with black suspenders. His chin is tucked down, and he's one of the few children not smiling. His dark eyes are clear and direct, peering out from beneath a shock of black hair. While I was in third grade in Mathis Elementary School, Pete was in pre-primer at Mathis West Ward School. West Ward was a one-room frame building where hispanic children had to stay until they learned English. Rumor was that the teacher had a big stick and would hit the kids if they spoke Spanish, but most of them never learned English there. Pete stayed in West Ward and never graduated from high school. He learned to get by.

After living at Knolle Jersey Farms for 20 years, Pete built his own house on property he'd bought in Sandia. There he and his wife Emma raised three daughters and three sons. He built houses on the property for his children's families.

I went to see Pete when Emma was dying. As I was walking out of her room, Pete showed me a keepsake, hanging on the wall of the living room. It was a paycheck for $24.00 for the first month he'd been employed by Knolle Jersey Farms. He'd never cashed it. He'd framed it instead.

In Ed's last years, I began to take over my father's position, and I became in charge of what is still called Knolle Jersey Farms. I have now come to respect Pete more than ever. He's 73 now, and he irrigates and keeps the brush down on our 5000 acres of South Texas ranch land. With my cousin, A.W., he works 500 head of beef cattle on horseback and hauls the calves to market. He keeps the old tractors, trucks, and water wells in shape. He's electrician, plumber, carpenter, mechanic, fence-repair expert, tractor driver, and cowhand.

Just a short while before my father died in 2010, I saw Pete in the process of laying strips of white caliche on each side of the long driveway up to Ed's house.

Fig. 71B Pedro Olivarez
Knolle Jersey Farms, 2012,
Photo by Kent Savage

"Pete, this is ridiculous," I complained. "Why does Ed have you wasting your time like this?"

"Oh no, it's my idea. I told him I thought it would look pretty, but I'm doing it for him so he can see to drive on his road."

A few years later I knew Pete was ready to retire. One day, I asked him if he knew anyone who would also be good at his job. "We don't want you to have to work so hard, Pete."

Pete shook his head, "There's nobody else who can do it all. Not anymore."

Appendices

Introduction

This book is finished. It's written from my heart because I've wanted you to know my family and our farm as I remember them.

Although my book is complete, the bookshelves in my hallway are still full of fat notebooks. Some have pages compiled by Mama's family about the Masons and the Owings. And some have material saved by her aunt, Lou Ella Buchanan Wade, about the Buchanans.

There's a whole section of bookshelves with notebooks of information from Daddy's family. Some of the notebooks have his mother's complete correspondence, beginning with her mother, Jane Durward. Four bulging notebooks contain historical research on my father's father, Almond Knolle, the Knolles, and the Scherrers. Others have Jennie and Almond's own personal letters.

And then there are hundreds of missives from Mama, written to her mother in San Antonio about life on the Wade Ranch and on Knolle Jersey Farms.

Many of the big notebooks contain newspaper clippings and magazine articles about Knolle Jersey Farms from the 1940s until the present day.

Should I write another book? Doing justice to the materials compiled by our family would take me more years than I have. But the notebooks provide valuable historical information and family stories that I can't leave out. So I've created timelines that weave the historical details with the written and oral history of my family. These timelines are included in the Appendices.

Appendices 1-2 provide timelines of my

maternal ancestors, the Masons, the Owings, and the Buchanans, as well as those of my paternal side, the Scherrers, Knolles, and Pearsons.

Appendix 3 provides the history of Knolle Jersey Farms.

Since good writers are plentiful in the Knolle family, I've added essays and poems written by four of them.

Appendix 4: Poems and a drawing from a large collection of poems, plays, and essay by Mary Margaret Knolle. .

Appendix 5: notes aboard Fata Morgana has 2 essays by my brother, Charles Knolle.

Appendix 6: Two of numerous poems and stories published by my cousin, Kathy Knolle Horrigan.

Appendix 7: "A Trip in the Buggy with Papa" was written by Mary Knolle Sims.

Appendix 1: The Owings, Masons, and Buchanans

The Owings and the Masons: Colonial Americans

Aunt Beth's house in San Antonio was small to hold so much. Aunt Beth was a naturalist. In those days people didn't create butterfly gardens for their Monarchs. They chloroformed them and pinned them in picture frames. But in spite of the dead butterflies, the house on 420 Berkshire was full of life.

In the 1950s, my maternal grandmother, Louise Mason Buchanan, lived in San Antonio with her sister, Elizabeth Mason Burleson, who was my Aunt Beth. Often relatives and neighbors and children my age were there when our family visited. My great-grandmother Mary (Mame) Mason was sometimes there too. Once when she and I took a nap together, we played a game to see who could touch her toes to the bottom of the bed.

In the center of Aunt Beth's house was a portrait of our important ancestor, John Calvin Mason, the Congressman. I was told stories about him and his wife, Anne Eliza Owings, who had received a "pint of jewels" from Louis Philippe, France's "Citizen King."

I was fascinated by the tales I heard there, but my grandmother Louise Mason Buchanan made little of them.

1769 Before the United States is created, the Masons are thriving in the Colony of Virginia. In this year, Colonel James Shirley Mason is born in

Spotsylvania County, Virginia, to Lt. John Mason and Anna Shirley. Col. James Shirley Mason will eventually marry Elizabeth Fishback, whose family immigrated to Virginia from Germany in 1714. James and Elizabeth will make their home in Mt. Sterling, Montgomery County, Kentucky and will have seven children.

Family stories say that James Shirley Mason "was very religious, would cut his own wood for fireplaces on Sunday rather than have slaves do any work on Sabbath Day." [2]

James Mason is a military man and holds the rank of Major under Governor Isaac Shelby of Kentucky. In the War of 1812, he leads a group of men who "fought in the rigging of ships, [as] sharpshooters."[3] The Masons will eventually be joined through marriage to the Owings of Baltimore.

1776   In this year of 1776, Col. Thomas Deye Owings is born at John and Thomas Forest, Maryland, the ancestral home of the Colegates, his mother's family. Like Col. James Shirley Mason, Owings will also serve in the War of 1812, but he makes his fortune by operating the first iron smelter located west of the Allegheny mountains.

Col. Owings will marry Maria Nicholas of Lexington, and they will have seven children, two of whom will die in infancy. Maria's mother comes from the well-known Smith family of Baltimore, who are ship owners and bankers and war heroes.[4] Maria's father was George Nicholas, "a member of the Virginia House of Delegates and First Professor of Law at Transylvania University in Lexington."[5]

1802   John Calvin Mason (son of Col. James Shirley Mason) is born near Mt. Sterling in

Montgomery County, Kentucky. John Calvin Mason will graduate from Mt. Sterling Law School and Transylvania University in Lexington, Kentucky, the first university west of the Mississippi.[6]

1812-1814   Col. Owings and his family are now in Kentucky where he builds a mansion in the soon-to-be-named town of Owingsville. The Owings family entertains a host of dignitaries including Henry Clay, who is a long-time friend.

Fig. 72 Owings House, Owingsville, KY, 1811-1814
for Col. Thomas Deye Owings by Benjamin Latrobe, who re-
designed the interior of the U.S. Capitol after the British
burned it, War of 1812. This house was the center of
Owingsville social life during the 1800's.

1814   One visitor, Louis Philippe, the French "Citizen King," spends a year at the Owings mansion. Upon departure, he expresses his gratitude by giving the Owings a "pint of jewels" which will later be distributed among the children and passed down through the generations.[7]

1836 Col. Owings responds to requests for men to fight in the Texas Revolution against Mexico. He offers to raise two regiments of troops from Kentucky. In a letter from New Orleans, dated January 18, 1936, Stephen F. Austin writes to him:

> Your offer to furnish one or more regiments not to exceed fifteen hundred men in all, to be in Texas by March next, for the struggle in which [Texas] is at present engaged, is thankfully received.[8]

1836 Col. Owings' son, Robert Smith Owings, is killed in the Goliad Massacre on March 27. Two of his cousins, Samuel Smith Saunders and N.B. Hawkins, are also killed in Goliad with Col. James Fannin's men. N. B. Hawkins was "a beardless youth not yet 16, the youngest victim of Santa Anna's butchery at Goliad."[9]

1842 Col. Owings' youngest daughter, Ann Eliza, marries John Calvin Mason, who has a working relationship with Owings in the business of iron-smelting. Ann Eliza and John Calvin Mason will have 13 children, eight of whom will die before the age of 14.

1847 John Calvin Mason serves in Ben McCullough's Company of Texas Rangers in the War with Mexico. After being wounded in the Battle of Monterrey, he "was sent to Washington, D. C. with dispatches to President Polk. He was appointed Quartermaster with the rank of Major in the service of the United States by President James K. Polk for gallantry on the field."[10]

Mason returns to Kentucky and is elected to the United States Congress as a Representative from Kentucky.

1861 Mason and his family are living in Kentucky, a slave state, as the Civil War begins. They live near the Ohio River, which is one of the boundaries between the North and the South, and so Mason moves his family to Brenham, Texas for their safety. He intends to return to Kentucky and raise troops for the Confederacy, but due to ill health, he stays in Texas.

1863 John Calvin Mason joins the Greybeards of the Texas State Troops in service of the Confederacy.[11]

1864-1865 John Calvin and Ann Eliza Mason both die in these years. On his way to Kentucky, John Calvin dies at 63 on the Mississippi River just above New Orleans. He is originally buried in New Orleans, but the Kentucky legislature orders that he be reinterred in the State Cemetery at Frankfurt.[12] Ann Eliza dies at 42 and is buried in Brenham, Texas.

1865 The two youngest Mason children, Robert Armistead and George, are four and five when their parents die. Their sister, Charcilla, becomes their guardian at 18 and raises them on a farm in Washington County, Texas.

1876 Robert Armistead Mason, now 15, is sent to live with a cousin in Owingsville, Kentucky. Later, he studies in his cousin's law office.

1883 Armistead Mason marries Mary Ruth Fassett in her father's home, Forest View, in Flat Creek, Bath County, Kentucky. The couple immediately leave for Brenham, Texas, where Armistead had been living.

The bride, Mary Ruth Fassett, is noted as being, "one of the fairest jewels in Bath's diadem of beauty and goodness. After a sumptuous repast, the happy couple came to this city [Mount Sterling, Kentucky] and took the 1:40 train to the Lone Star State, followed by the good wishes of hundreds of friends."[13] The couple eventually have eight children, one child will die at five months of age.

Armistead's brother, George marries Mary Ruth Fassett's sister Elizabeth (Lizzie) Adelaide. They will have nine children, and Elizabeth will die in childbirth along with the baby, Ann Eliza.

1885 Armistead and George move with their families to West Texas, eventually settling in Haskell. Armistead runs a saloon, and George runs a merchandise and grocery store. Later, George buys a racehorse from Kentucky and begins horse racing.

1893 Armistead shoots and kills a man. A relative of Armistead's will later say, "He was a man who needed killing."[14] Armistead and Mary Ruth move to Kentucky before the trial, and they remain in Kentucky for the next 12 years.

George leaves Texas as well. He "sells everything and goes to the 'Mountains of Kentucky,' where he tries to reclaim his property from squatters. He builds a log cabin, holds court in the yard, and is given White's Hollow."[15]

Fig. 73 Families of George and Armistead Mason, White's Hollow in the mountains of Kentucky, July 1895
l. to r., Charcilla Owings (Chess Jr.), Robert, George, Elizabeth, Armistead holding Seth, unknown older male, Sarah (Sade), Roger, George holding Thomas

1900 George is persuaded by a cousin to move to Puntagordo, British Honduras, to run a plantation store, and he moves his family once again.

1902 In Puntagordo, George's wife, Lizzie, dies at age 41 in childbirth with their 8th child, Ann Eliza. Of their eight children, only five survive to maturity. George dies five years later and is buried in Brenham, Texas.

1905 Armistead, now 44, and Mary Ruth, now 38, move their family from Kentucky to San Antonio, Texas. Louise Mason is their 6th child.

1917 Louise Mason graduates from Main High School in San Antonio. Her oldest brother John Calvin writes a congratulatory letter to her from his bank office in Dallas:

> My dear little Sis;
> We received your graduation announcement and I assure you that the fact that you are finishing high school gives no one more pride and satisfaction, unless it be Elizabeth, to whose kind help you owe being able to, than your big brother.[16]

1917-1920 Louise meets Floyd Buchanan, who's a cadet at San Antonio Military Academy. By the time Floyd enlists in the U.S. armed services on May 16, 1917, Louise and Floyd are in love. He is discharged March 29, 1919, and they marry on March 29, 1920, in El Paso, Texas.

1931-1942 Louise and Floyd live in North Texas until 1931 when they move with their daughter, Mary Margaret, to Floyd's home on the Wade Ranch in South Texas. The years that follow are painful and difficult for Floyd and Louise, and Floyd dies early at 46. Louise is left a widow with only a small pension.

1945-1960 Louise Mason Buchanan now lives with her sister Elizabeth Mason Burleson whose home in San Antonio has become the headquarters for the Mason family. The small house on the south side of town is often filled with their Mason brothers and sisters and children. The 100-year oil portrait of John Calvin Mason, the Congressman, hangs on the dining room wall.

Robert Armisted Mason Family

Armistead Mason (1861-1923)
m.
Mary Ruth Fassett (1864-1951)

John Calvin (1884) m. Irma Conley	Woodman Fassett (1887) died 1889
George Nicholas (1889)	Elizabeth Hanson (1890) m. James C. Burleson
Seth Shepard (1895) m. Ernestine Hoggatt	Clara Louise (1897) m. Floyd Buchanan
Charles Owings (1899)	Anna Elise (1904) m. Ray Pyland

Robert Armistead Mason and his brother George Mason married two sisters, Mary Ruth Fassett and Elizabeth Adelaide Fassett.

John Calvin Mason's wife, Irma Conley died, leaving him with six young children. His mother Mary Ruth Fassett raised his six children, her second large family.

Mary Ruth Fassett was affectionately called "Mame" by her grandchildren, a name Mary Margaret Knolle later chose for herself as a grandmother.

Sanford and Pinkie Buchanan: To Texas from the Old South

The portraits are ugly. Pre-Civil War etchings of two plain women. The women are dressed in black high-neck shirtwaists. Their black hair is center-parted and pulled straight back. They look directly forward, and neither is smiling. The etchings are framed in heavy, dark wood.

The women in the etchings are Arminta Ezell Bumpass Buchanan and Phoebe Titus Crawford Buchanan. They were two of my mother's great-grandmothers. The portraits once hung over the mantle in the Big House at the Wade Ranch. After Mama got them, she put them in the back of her bedroom closet.

In the 1830's, Arminta Ezell Bumpas and Phoebe Titus Crawford married two Buchanans. Not surprisingly, Phoebe and Arminta could also be traced back to the Buchanans of Lincoln County, Tennessee. At that time, it was common for cousins to marry, and large families were the norm. Phoebe gave birth to Sanford McElroy Buchanan, and Arminta gave birth to Margaret Pinkie Buchanan. Sanford and Margaret Pinkie, second cousins, married in 1875 in Fayetteville, Tennessee. They were Mama's grandparents.

The name "Pinkie" was often used among the Buchanans of that time. It has an historical reference to the Battle of Pinkie Cluegh when the Clan Buchanan fought against the English in the Scottish Lowlands in 1547. For the Scots, this disastrous battle is known as Black Saturday.[17]

Sanford and Pinkie had grown up on nearby plantations in Lincoln County near Fayetteville. Sanford studied at East Tennessee University in

Lincoln County, but the devastation and lack of opportunity caused by the Civil War led him and Pinkie in 1877 to pack up their one-year-old child, Lou Ella, and go to Texas in search of a better life. They were the first Buchanans to leave Lincoln County.

1877 Sanford and Pinkie and little Lou Ella move to Corsicana in East Texas, then to Midway (Midland), and finally settle near Fort Worth, in Weatherford, Navarro County, Texas.

Sanford does the work he knows, sharecropping and farming. Seven more children will be born to Pinkie and Sanford as they move throughout Texas: after Lou Ella, Tom, Della, Arminta, Myrtle, Ezella, Sanford Roy, and Simmons will be born. Sanford Roy will die before he is two years old.

1893 In this year, Sanford and Pinkie move their family to Rockport, in South Texas where their ninth child, Gordon, is born. The Buchanans continue southward by covered wagon toward the Lower Nueces River Valley. They move onto the Wade Ranch where Sanford helps the owner, John Wade, plant extensive acreage in watermelons.[18]

Fig. 74 John Wade's watermelon crop put in by Sanford Buchanan, circa 1890s

1894 Sanford and Pinkie's oldest daughter, Lou Ella, is now 18, and she marries Wallis Wade, the son of John Wade. Wallis will inherit most of the Wade Ranch in three years.

Lou Ella and Wallis live first in the original Wade Ranch house while they design and build the Big House which will become the center of the Wade Ranch. The Big House is Victorian-style, surrounded by screened-in porches. There are columns in the entry hall, mantles with mirrors, a music room, and a staircase in the dining room. Family stories talk about a secret hiding place underneath the elegant staircase, recessed into the dark wood paneling. Everybody knew important things were kept there.

1895 In August of this year, Lou Ella gives birth to a baby boy who dies hours later. Lou Ella nearly dies as well, and she is never able to have another child.

1896 In the spring Lou Ella's mother Pinkie

gives birth to her 10th child, Floyd. Lou Ella and Wallis take Floyd into their care and will raise him on the Wade Ranch as their own son.

1916 Floyd attends Texas Military Institute in San Antonio, then known as West Texas Military Academy. While he is in San Antonio, he meets and falls in love with Louise Mason.

1917 On May 16th, Floyd enlists in the American Expeditionary Forces in World War I at the age of 21. He will rise to the rank of sergeant of Battery A, 131 Field Artillery of the 36th Division.[19] Floyd's daughter later will write that he "went to France where he was in charge of a prisoner of war camp for German captives. He was very popular with his charges; I remember his collection of hand carved gifts and other memorabilia which his appreciative prisoners made for him."[20]

1919 Floyd returns to Camp Travis [now part of Fort Sam Houston] in San Antonio and receives an Honorable Discharge from the United States Army on March 29, 1919.[21]

1920 Floyd Buchanan and Louise Mason marry in El Paso, Texas. They will live in North Texas for the next ten years where Floyd will work as a District Manager for Wilson and Company, Meat Packers and Distributors.

1921 A daughter Mary Margaret is born to Floyd and Louise in July of this year. She will be their only child.

1926 Floyd's father Sanford Buchanan dies at

age 72 at his home on Shell Road in Corpus Christi. Floyd's mother Pinkie Buchanan is taken in by Lou Ella and Wallis. Pinkie moves to the Wade Ranch where she will live behind the Big House until her death 25 years later.

1931 Lou Ella tries to persuade Floyd to quit his job with the Wilson Company after Wallis has had a slight stroke. Lou Ella insists that she needs help running the Wade Ranch and assures Floyd he will inherit the Ranch after her death.[22] Floyd finally agrees, and he moves with Louise and Mary Margaret to the Ranch where they will live with his mother, Pinkie, behind the Big House. Floyd and Louise will both work for Lou Ella but will never receive a salary.[23]

1932-1937 Trouble develops quickly for Floyd and Louise. Lou Ella is controlling of Floyd and fiercely jealous of Louise and Mary Margaret. Their family life is unbearable.[24] Louise frequently visits her family in San Antonio, and Mary Margaret goes to live with her Aunt Ezella in Corpus Christi in order to complete high school.

Mary Margaret marries Edward Knolle secretly in September, 1937. She is 16, and he is 25. She moves to Sandia with Ed in the spring of 1938 after she graduates from high school.

1938-42 Floyd tries to find employment off the Wade Ranch but doesn't succeed. His friends get him positions, but Lou Ella always talks Floyd into staying.[25] Louise eventually finds employment in San Antonio as a practical nurse, living and caring for patients in their homes.[26]

1942 Floyd has been in poor health for some

time and unexpectedly dies of a stroke in the Mathis
hospital at 46.

Sanford Buchanan Family

Sanford Buchanan (1853-1956)
m.
Margaret Pinkie Buchanan (1857-1951)

Lou Ella (1876) m Wallis Wade	Tom (1877) m Adelaide Williams	Della (1880) m Roy Page	Arminta (1883) m Rolly Atkinson
Myrtle (1885) m Sam Rountree	Ezella (1886) m James Priestly	Sanford Roy (1889) Died in infancy	Simmons (1890) m Ruth Drewth
	Gordon (1895) m Bessie Butler	Floyd (1896) m Louise Mason	

Sanford and Pinkie Buchanan were second cousins.

Lou Ella's and Wallis's baby died at birth within the same year that Floyd was born. Lou Ella and Wallis raised her parents' last child, Floyd, on the Wade Ranch, as their own son.

Appendix 2: The Scherrers, Knolles, and Pearsons

Bernard Scherrer: Citizen of the Republic of Texas

My mother Mary Margaret had a plan. It was the only time my father Ed said no to her, except for when he'd made her quit taking flying lessons before she'd had a chance to solo.

Mama wanted to purchase Bernard Scherrer's log cabin in Biegel, Texas, because he was Ed's great-grandfather. She wanted to move it 170 miles to our farm in Sandia and restore it as a Knolle family museum. The log house would be dismantled, and each old log would be numbered to correspond to an architectural diagram that would be followed when the house was rebuilt.

If I'd been asked my opinion, I'd have agreed with Daddy. Moving the house would have been a hopelessly complicated and expensive procedure. The house Mama wanted to purchase and restore was the one Bernard Scherrer had built in 1845 for his bride, Gesine.

But Mama didn't get the house, and in 1976, the Scherrer homestead, its family cemetery, and the entire town of Biegel was covered by a lake created by the Fayette County Power Project.

I've often wondered why Mama was so interested in Bernard Scherrer and why she'd wanted to attempt this project. I know that in 1974, she and Ed and his sister Katherine took a trip to Biegel and visited the owners of the Scherrer homestead. They took photographs, discovered artifacts, and Mama would later write extensively about the history she'd learned on the trip.

Later, Mama developed a friendship with Julia Collins, Ed's cousin and also Bernard Scherrer's great-grandchild. Julia was doing research to get a DAR marker for Scherrer's grave. I put together the following timeline from Mary Margaret's writings, notes, and correspondence.

1807 Bernard Scherrer is born on August 20th in St. Gallen, northeastern Switzerland where the Swiss-German dialect is spoken. He receives a university education in St. Gallen.

1829 Bernard Scherrer is 22 when he emigrates from St. Gallen to New York. His Swiss passport is dated November 19 and establishes that he "est intentionne d'aller pour des affaires de commerce on Amerique."[27] He embarks at Le Havre, France on the ship France and arrives in New York on February 4, 1830, a 2-month journey.

1830 After arriving in New York, he spends time there and then begins to travel extensively. He travels to Quebec, up the St. Lawrence River to Buffalo, over the Great Lakes, and on to St. Louis, Missouri by stage. He goes from St. Louis to New Orleans by way of the Mississippi River. [28]

1833 In New Orleans, Scherrer meets a German explorer Detlef Dunt and travels to Texas with him on the schooner *Sabine*. Dunt will soon return to Germany and publish an account of his travels in *Reise Nach Texas* [Journey to Texas], the first German book about Texas.[29]

After the *Sabine* reaches Brazoria, Scherrer

meets with Henry Smith, the Alcalde of the State of Texas and Coahuila, and obtains a Mexican passport. The passport gives him permission "para que pase de esta a qualquier punto de la Republica." As well, the passport gives him protection. "Pido las autoridades civile y como militares que lo deje pasas sin embarago alguno."[30]

Scherrer isn't favorably impressed with the territory under the rule of Mexico, so he and Charles Fordtran, an immigrant from Alsace-Lorraine, travel to St. Louis. Not finding that land to their liking, they return to Texas on horseback. Scherrer and Fordtran arrive at Johann Friedrich Ernst's settlement on the banks of Mill's Creek in Stephen F. Austin's colony. Fordtran had previously established himself in the Mill's Creek area with Ernst.

Tradition goes that Scherrer taught the Ernsts cigar-making during the noon hours. Their neighbors, the Fordtran family, preferred to rest at noon and jokingly called the Ernsts "The Industrious Ones," who in turn called the Fordtrans "The Indolent Ones." It can be said that the historic town of Industry received its name because of Bernard Scherrer's endeavors.[31]

Scherrer meets Joseph Biegel, who convinces him to become a partner in his plans for a second German settlement. Biegel and his wife couldn't read or write, so Scherrer is more than likely a major asset to the development of the settlement with his university education.[32]

1836 Scherrer, now 29, joins the John York Company of Colonel Edward Burleson's regiment to fight in the Texas Revolution.[33] It is said "that Scherrer was a ranger and scout for General Sam Houston, obtaining beef for the soldiers and protecting families during the Runaway Scrape."[34]

In the Battle of San Jacinto, Houston orders Colonel Burleson, Scherrer's commander, to place his regiment opposite the Mexican breastworks and be the first to charge. Family stories say that Scherrer is sent to scout for supplies and misses the 18-minute battle.

Fig. 75 Crib House
restored and moved to Round Top, Texas, 1986

1838 Two years after the war, Scherrer buys 1,125 acres of land for $500.00 from his friend Joseph Biegel. Scherrer first lives in a small log cabin called the Crib House that is on the land he's purchased. He becomes a cotton planter and a waggoneer. Using oxen to pull his wagons, he hauls goods to and from the ports of Galveston and Indianola.

Scherrer is appointed by Sam Houston, now President of the Republic of Texas, to be the first

Justice of the Peace for the third district of Fayette County.[35]

1840 The 1840 Census of the Republic of Texas credits Scherrer with over 2,500 acres of land, one saddle horse, and 16 cattle.

1842 In this year and again in 1847, Scherrer is appointed County Commissioner to oversee all roads from Biegel to Rutersville and within Fayette County.[36]

1845 Scherrer, now 38, marries Gesine Elisa Margaret Koch, aged 18, in Industry. Gesine had been born in Oldenburg, Germany in 1827 and had immigrated to Texas with her family. After their wedding, Bernard and Gesine ride on horseback to a double-log house which he's built for her in the Biegel Settlement. They will have seven children, one of whom dies at age 23.[37]
Scherrer develops a freighting business, is a planter of cotton, and becomes a prominent leader of the settlement of Biegel and of Fayette County. He builds the first school in Fayette County for his children and the children of neighboring families.[38]

1861 At the age of 54, Scherrer serves the Confederacy in a volunteer unit, the Dixie Greys.[39]

1872 On Christmas Day, Bernard and Gesine's third daughter, Mary Eliza Scherrer, marries Ernst Paul Knolle of Industry. Mary Eliza's older sister, Caroline, has already married Ernst Paul's brother Hermann Knolle. Mary Scherrer and Ernst Paul move to Flatonia.

1880 Mary is widowed at 27 when Ernst Paul

dies of typhoid fever. She has two children, Buena Vista, seven years, and Almond, five, and she is pregnant with their third child, Lee.

Soon after Ernst Paul's death, Mary moves to a house on Austin Street in San Antonio. The small, two-story, rock house with an outside staircase will be a landmark in downtown San Antonio until it is torn down in the 1960s to make way for Hemisfair.[40]

The house on Austin Street is near the yards (the depot and train station). Almond is allowed to roam San Antonio at an early age. "His first job was cleaning out boxcars at the train station, and he was a fleet-footed cash boy in Wolfson's Department Store. He rode the rails with Coxey's army of unemployed[41] and in 1886, shook the hand of the notorious Apache Chief, Geronimo[42] who was a prisoner . . . chained to a box car."[43]

In San Antonio, Mary Scherrer Knolle makes "overalls for men and for a factory in San Antonio. She [would] pick up pre-cut material[s]"[44] and sew them into overalls. Mary is hardworking and thrifty, but it is probably with the help of her wealthy father that she is able to buy a permanent home for her family at 1711 West French Place.

Family stories say that "Oma [Mary Scherrer Knolle] was born in a log cabin and grew up with a love of the soil and knowledge of crops and cattle. While still a young girl she had learned to use a spinning wheel and a sharpshooter, as the occasion demanded . . . But a long life of toil did not bring a stoop to her tall erect frame nor take the note of cheerfulness from her voice . . ."[45]

"Her dearest possession was an accordion on which she had learned to play by ear as a girl. At the age of seventy-five she could still get lively tunes from it, as her feet tapped time and her eyes shone with happy memories."[46]

1885 Almond, at the age of nine, makes a train trip alone from San Antonio to La Grange to visit his grandparents, Gisene and Bernard Scherrer. Arriving at the railroad depot in La Grange, Almond makes his way to the Beigel Settlement on his own.

When Almond finally gets to the house, Gisene, who hasn't seen him in four years, doesn't recognize her grandson and refuses to let him in until he identifies himself. When he does so, she swings open the kitchen door and engulfs him in her arms.

Almond then finds his grandfather in the blacksmith shed, repairing a wheel, and Bernard doesn't recognize Almond either. Almond spends two weeks with his grandparents. He will later say that it seemed to him that his grandfather worked on that one wagon wheel the entire time.[47]

1892 Bernard Scherrer dies at age 85 at the Scherrer homestead in Biegel.

1904 Gesine Sherrer, dies at age 77. Gesine and Bernard's two unmarried children will live the rest of their lives on the Scherrer homestead with Anna dying in 1935 and August dying in 1926.

1935 Mary Scherrer Knolle dies at the age of 82 at her home on West French Place. Her daughter, Buena Vista, will continue to live in their home until her death in 1963.

1978 Fayette County builds a new dam on the Lower Colorado River, the entire town of Biegel and much surrounding land is inundated by water. The remains of Bernard and Gesine Koch Scherrer, their son Heinrich, and Gesine's mother, Margaret Koch, are moved from a private cemetery on the Scherrer homestead and reinterred at the La Grange Cemetery.[48]

1986 In April of this year, the Daughters of the Republic of Texas, sponsored by Julia Meinart Collins, place a plaque on his grave, naming him a Citizen of the Republic of Texas.

In September, fifty descendants of Bernard Scherrer gather at Scherrer's Crib House, now located at Henkel Square in Round Top, to celebrate his contributions to Texas.

1993 Bernard Scherrer is memorialized with a Texas Historical Marker by the Fayette County Historical Society in a ceremony at Henkel Square, Round Top.

Bernard Scherrer Family

Bernard Scherrer (1807-1892)
m.
Gesine Eliza Koch (1827-1904)

Henrich (1847-1870)	Anna (1851-1935)
No issue	No issue
August (1849-1926)	Caroline (1846-1874) m. Herman Knolle
No issue	Bernard Ernest Edmond Robert Albert Pleasant Arnold August Herman Odine
Mary (1853-1935) m. Ernst Paul Knolle	Emelia (1856-1931) m. Cornelius Gehrels
Buena Vista Almond Henry Raymond Lee	William John Anna Ella

Julia (1862-1923)
m.
William Mienert

Bernard
Alfred
Alma
Lawrence

The Knolles: The Industrious Ones

The Knolle family can be traced to Stadthagen, Germany as far back as the 30 Years' War (1618-1648) "when the Swedes were occupying and fighting in the area."[49] It may be that the Knolles came from Sweden.

Ernst G. Knolle, who lived in California, would tell this story. Once he was traveling in Denmark, a "Danish customs official . . . asked whether [my] forefathers originated in Scandinavia. Frankly, we were surprised. [The official] said he was from Sweden and that Knolle was a common name in his hometown."[50] We begin here with the first Knolles to immigrate to Texas from Stadthagen, Germany, Ernst Friedrich Gottlieb Knolle (Ernst F. G.) and Dorothea Frederika Charlotte Eleanore Brandt (Doris).

1837 Ernst F. G. Knolle marries Doris Brandt on December 24, in Petzen, Germany. Ernst F. G., a schoolteacher, is 24, and Doris is 26. Through the years, Doris will give birth to six children, two of whom will die in infancy in Germany.

1844 Ernst F. G. and Doris immigrate with their two children, Herminia Wilhelmina Sophia, age two, and Hermann Ernst, an infant. They make their way to Industry, Texas.

Traveling with the Knolle family is Christof Kubitz from Prussia. Census records will show that Kubitz lives with the Knolles for several years. He will marry Ernst F. G. and Doris' daughter Sophia in 1856.

Ernst F.G. is the ship's preacher on the passage from Germany to New York. He's "Lutheran, not an ordained priest, but an 'exhorter' who preaches both aboard the ship and after he makes a life in Texas."[51]

1848 Two of Ernst F. G.'s brothers follow him and immigrate to Industry as well. Ernst F. G.'s older brother, Anton Friedrich Gottlieb (Fritz), comes with his family and their widowed mother Philippine. The second brother, Anton Wilhelm Christian, immigrates to Industry with his two sons. After the Civil War, Anton Wilhem and his sons will move to Ohio. Only one of the brothers Johann Heinrich Knolle stays on the Knolle farm near Stadthagan, in the village of Krebshagan, Schaumberg-Lippe, Germany.

Ernst F. G. and Doris have their first child born in America, Emil Moses Ernst Knolle.

1854 Ernst F. G. and Doris' youngest child, Ernst Paul Knolle, is born in this year. Ernst Paul will become the father of Almond Henry Knolle.

1850's Ernst F. G.'s sense of purpose and his physical strength help him create financial success. Eventually, he'll become a leading citizen of the town of Industry.

Ernst F. G. and his brother Fritz begin buying land. "Between 1846 and 1850," they purchase "3,000 acres of the John F. Pettus league." By the 1850's, cotton is the area's major crop along with tobacco, and Ernst F. G. sees these crops as an avenue to wealth.[52]

During this decade, Ernst F. G. becomes "a prominent, prosperous planter and owner of 90 male slaves. He owned and operated a tannery, flour and grist mills, a lumber mill and a cotton gin."[53] It's been said that "he possessed great energy and determination, was wiry and sinewy and accomplished feats of endurance that few men would undertake. He was wont to ride his favorite saddler to Houston during a night, buy his goods in the markets the next day, and ride back to Industry again, 65 miles that night, and be ready for business the next morning."[54]

1861-65 During this period of the Civil War, Ernst F. G. suffers financial ruin and family tragedies. "Mr. Knolle was a fiery secessionist and supported the Confederacy with his own money." He believed so much in the Confederate army that he put all his money into Confederate bonds, and "the fall of the Lost Cause was a severe blow to him, and all his property was swept away."[55]

1862 Ernst F. G.'s oldest son, Hermann, enlists in Voigt's Confederate Legion at age 18 with his brother-in-law Dr. Christof Kubitz and two of his cousins, Friedrich (Fred) Knolle and Henry Brandt.[56] They're first sent to Houston where they stay about six weeks. Before leaving Texas, Hermann is given a 10-day furlough and goes home to see his family in Industry.

Hermann comes down with the measles as soon as he gets home. Hermann's sister (Christof's wife), Sofia Knolle Kubitz, catches the measles from him. The three Kubitz children also come down with the disease, and the mother and children all die within weeks of each other.[57]

1863 Dr. Christof Kubitz is captured after the Battle of Vicksburg in July and escapes by swimming across the Yazoo River. Many think he has drowned, but he survives, marries again, and has several children before he dies in 1873.

Hermann and his cousin Fred are captured near Vicksburg and imprisoned at Camp Morton near Indianapolis where Fred dies of pneumonia. He's just 22.[58]

1865 On Feb. 25, Hermann is part of a prisoner exchange and is released. He will write later, "words cannot express the joy I felt as I walked out of the gate and was at last once more on the road to be free."

Hermann's seven-month journey home is marked by starvation and unsanitary conditions. He writes, "Our rations were 1 cracker to the man, and some pickle beef which we had no chance to cook. A great number of the men were starved on the [train] trip. Each man is hardly allowed room enough to sit down from the first to the last day."[59]

Hermann walks the last 300 or so miles of the journey home and makes it back to Industry on September 4. He soon marries Caroline Scherrer, and they have five sons together. But the war has broken Hermann's health, and he will die in his father's arms at age 29.[60]

1872 Hermann's younger brother, Ernst Paul, is now 19, and he marries Caroline Scherrer Knolle's sister, Mary Eliza Scherrer. Mary and Caroline are the daughters of Bernard Scherrer, who has been a major force in the development of Fayette County and the town of Biegel.

1873 By this time, Ernst F. G.'s wife Doris has died. He marries Caroline Justine (Augusta) Wilhelmine Moeschen nee Moller, a distant cousin who is a Civil War widow with four daughters. Ernst F.G. and Augusta will have a son Arthur Ernst who will someday live in Corpus Christi with his daughter Dorothy. Arthur Ernst will be known affectionately as Uncle Arthur to Almond Knolle and his family.

1874 Hermann's wife Caroline Scherrer Knolle

dies a year after his death, leaving their young boys orphaned. Hermann's younger brother, Emil Ernst Moses, and his wife Ernestine become the children's guardians. They provide an education for them as they do for their own children.

Three of Hermann's sons will become medical doctors along with three of Emil's sons, beginning a long tradition of Knolle doctors in Texas.

Ernst F. G. is now 63. On May 30 of this year, he writes to his brother, Johann Heinrich Knolle, who had stayed in Germany. "Of the members of my family who came to Texas with me, I am the only survivor. The good Doris, the lovely Herminia, her three children, also Kubitz, my son-in-law, my son, Hermann, all left for a far country from whence no wanderer returns."[61]

Ernst F. G. divides his remaining farm between his sons Emil Moses and Ernst Paul and becomes a businessman in Brenham where he lives in a small house and has "the largest, most beautiful store."[62]

1880 Ernst Frederick Gottlieb Knolle dies on Oct 22, at the age of 67. Right after Ernst F. G.'s death, his son Ernst Paul dies of typhoid fever. Ernst Paul Knolle is only 25 and leaves his widow, Mary Scherrer Knolle, with two young children, Buena Vista (7) and Almond Henry (5). Mary is pregnant with another child, Raymond Lee, who will be born in 1881.

Mary moves to San Antonio where she'll raise her three children. Almond roams the city at an early age. His first job is cleaning out boxcars at the Sunset train station.[63]

In later years, Almond will claim that he only went to fifth grade. However, throughout his life, he reads the classics, keeps up an extensive correspondence with business associates, even giving advice to city officials whom he thinks need some better ideas. He also writes articles about beekeeping and farming.[64]

1900 Almond marries Jennie Pearson on September 20, 1900. They'll eventually live on a farm in Sandia, Texas, and have eight children.

1913 By this year, Almond is supporting his large family with bees and farming his 400 acres. He receives a letter from Dr. F. M. Hicks who had helped him earlier in his life. Dr. Hicks writes from San Antonio on July 7, "It always gives me pleasure to think of you. I am proud of the part I played in helping you get on your feet. You remember that you said that if I could get you so that you could walk that you would not need or want help from anyone. You certainly have made good."[65]

Almond Knolle grows up with no father and no father figure to teach him about his paternal family, but he embodies and passes on to his children the Knolle traits of perseverance and determination and faith in himself.

Ernst F.G. Knolle Family	
Ernst F.G. Knolle (1812-1889 ***m.*** **Dorothea Brandt (1811-1867)**	
Sofia Wilhelmina (1842-1862) ***m.*** **Christof Kubitz** **Sofia and their 3 Children die of measles in 1862**	**Herman (1844-1873)** ***m.*** **Caroline Knolle** **Bernard Ernest** **Edmond Robert** **Albert Pleasant** **Arnold August** **Herman Odine**
Emil (1848-1931) ***m.*** **Ernestine Wiese** **Nora** **Zulie** **Otto (Jack)** **Jessie** **Benny** **Kinch C**	**Ernst Paul (1854-1880)** ***m.*** **Mary Scherrer** **Buena Vista** **Almond Henry** **Raymond Lee**

Dorothea Knolle dies in 1868. Ernst F.G. marries Justine Moller Boeschen in 1872. They have one child together, Arthur Ernest Knolle ("Uncle Arthur" to Almond's family). Herman Knolle and his wife Caroline Scherrer Knolle die in 1873 and 1874. Emil and Ernestine Knolle take in their five orphaned nephews and raise them with their own six children.

Almond Knolle Family	
Almond Knolle (1875-1969)	
m.	
Jennie Knolle (1876-1972)	
Mary (1901)	Katherine (1903)
m.	
Horace Sims	
Henry (1906)	Arthur (1908)
m	m.
. Florence Mahoney	Grace Davis
Pearson	Carolyn
Joe	Susan
Bob (1910)	Ed (1912)
m.	m.
Adele Huvar	Mary Margaret
	Buchanan
Ginny	
	Louise
	Charles
Ruth (1915)	Walton (1917)
m.	m.
LeRoy Lain	Dorothy Beall
Janice	A.W.
Margaret	Kathy
Tom	

The Pearsons: To Texas from Scotland by way of India

Jennie Pearson and her family immigrated from Scotland to America in 1881 when she was only five years old, a good 40 years later than Almond Knolle's German grandfathers in the 1840's.

The Pearsons found a different world in the 1880's. The Texas that Peter Pearson and Jane Durward Pearson encountered was no longer a frontier. Texas had endured wars with Mexico and the Civil War. By the 1880's, the cattle drives were mostly over, and railroads were linking Texas towns. Throughout most of the U.S., the industrial revolution was re-shaping America.

Peter and Jane Pearson weren't frontier pioneers. But life in this next era of South Texas was no easier than early frontier life. The Pearsons found that neither a knowledge of Latin nor the ability to make fine hand-sewn lace was valued in their new world.

I've intertwined the stories of Peter Pearson and Jane Durward, Jennie's father and mother, because I can't separate them. The immigrant story of Peter and Jane belongs to them together. Theirs is a story of endurance and terrible loss, a story of faith and resilience.

1841 Jennie's father, Peter Pearson, is born in the parish of Brechin, Forfarshire, Kinecardineshire, Scotland. Peter is the third son of Elizabeth Birrell Pearson and James Pearson, a farm overseer of 264 acres and nine laborers.

1855 Jennie's mother Jane Durward is born in

the parish of Fetteresso in Kincardineshire, Scotland. Jane is one of the 11 children of Jane Sparks Durward and David Durward, a farmer in Fetterosso.

1855 Peter is 14 when he begins working for David Craig as an accounts clerk in the parish of Brechin.

1859 At the age of 18, Peter receives a Letter of Reference from David Craig recommending Peter for a clerk position (accounts). Craig writes, "I have found him particularly steady, attentive and honest. He copies correctly, keeps correct accounts, and is a good arithmetician, besides having, as I know (for I have tested him) a very fair education in Latin."[66]

1866 Peter Pearson is now 25, and he receives a Letter of Reference from Adam Mitching, Minister of Little Cairn of "The Manse" in Fettercairn. The minister has known Peter for seven years and refers to him as "a young man of unreproachable character."[67]
In the same year, Peter also receives a Letter of Reference from Chas. Buril, a farmer of Dallaris by Edzell, who has known Peter for 11 years. Buril attests to him as being, "a steady trustworthy young man, very regular in his habits."[68]

1869 The Suez Canal opens on November 17. Family stories say that Peter Pearson is on the first passenger ship to pass through the Canal to India.[69]

1870 On April 1, Peter signs a contract for four years to "continue" managing and overseeing the Closeburn Estate, a coffee plantation in Mercara Coorg, an area in southwestern India. Peter will be working for two prominent Scots. James Kirkpatrick is a "Doctor of Medicine, Surgeon in Her Majesty's Indian Medical Service Madras Establishment." George Matthew Martin is a "retired Major of the East Indian Army Madras Establishment."[70]

The district of Coorg is called "The Scotland of India." "Most of the planters were Scots, and the uncanny similarities between both places earned Coorg that nickname. Like Scotland, Coorg is mountainous, misty, and cool."[71]

1874 Family stories say that Jane Durward's friends tease her and say that Peter will come home from India and marry her.[72] As it turns out, Peter does return and does marry Jane Durward. Jane comes from a large and loving family who live on an adjoining farm. Peter and Jane are married in West Drumhendry, Parish of Fettercairn, Kincardineshire, Scotland, on August 28. He is 33; she is 19. Peter's oldest brother, Andrew, and Jane's closest sister in age, Mary, are the witnesses.

Right after the wedding, Peter and Jane leave for Mercara Coorg where Peter will continue his management of the Closeburn coffee plantation. Durward family members still have the letter that one of Jane's brothers writes to India the morning after the wedding celebration, telling Jane about all the fun they'd had after Peter and Jane left.[73]

1875 Peter and Jane are photographed together in Bangalore, India. "This is the only picture of Peter. His look of strong determination is tempered by his uneasy effort to conceal his right hand from which two fingers were missing because of a gun accident in India."[74]

1876 Peter and Jane have their first child. Jane

Elizabeth (Jennie) Pearson is born on March 5 in Mercara Coorg.

The Pearsons become concerned about the civil uprisings against British rule in Southern India and decide to return to Scotland with Jennie, who is only months old. The Pearsons receive a birth certificate signed by the midwife who delivered Jennie.

1878 The second child of Peter and Jane, Margaret Durward (Maggie) Pearson, is born on May 28, in Drumoak, Aberdeenshire, Scotland.

1879 Their third child, Catherine Sarah Pearson, is born on August 8, in Drumoak as well.

1881 Their fourth child, George Pearson, is born on June 30, in the parish of Fetteresso, Kincardineshire.

1878-1881 Peter and his older brother Andrew have a disagreement over a land settlement connected to the death of their father in 1876. Peter is angry about the settlement, and he and Jane decide to immigrate to America.[75]

Advertisements in Scottish newspapers, promising "land grants to persons willing to sail across the Atlantic."[76] Family stories also recount that to immigrate, Peter and Jane sell all their treasures—among them an Indian fan made of elephant tusks and their cherished books.[77] They "are lured by a land shark who promises cheap land around Seguin, Texas."[78]

The Pearsons immigrate to America in the summer of 1881 on a ship from Liverpool, England. With them are their four young children Jennie, five, Maggie, three, Sarah (Katie), two, and George, an infant. Years later, Jennie will tell about leaving Scotland on a boat, waving to their kinsmen on the shore and singing 'Auld Lang Syne' until they could no longer hear one another."[79]

Family stories tell about the "storm in the Bay of Biscay during which Peter and Jane each held a baby for three days." The five year-old Jennie made friends with a five year-old boy "on the boat going to America. They would hang over the rail of the boat and watch the waves and have long talks together."[80]

1881 The Pearson's first experiences in their new world will be the odd food, hot weather, financial insecurity, and tragedy. After arriving in New York, it was common for new immigrants to stay at boarding houses.

"Jane ... told an amusing story about their stay in a New York boarding house. Some of them had never seen cornbread. On the dinner table were platters of hot cornbread which the Scots decided was yellow layer cake cut in squares. They decided Americans had strange dietary habits to eat dessert cake along with a meal like bread. They very carefully laid their pieces to one side to be eaten as dessert. Jane said they never forgot the shock of their first taste of cornbread, and neither she nor Peter ever learned to like it."[81]

From New York, Peter and Jane with the four children take a train to Boston and find some kind Scots to help them. When they arrive in Boston, Peter finds employment at a Boston dry goods store, owned by a Scot who favors his earnest countrymen immigrants. Jane cuts up her prized household linen and makes cooler clothes for her four little children to wear in the unaccustomed heat of summer. Soon they are financially able to proceed by train to Seguin,

Texas.[82]

"Their seats on the train from Boston had just been vacated by another family with small children who were very sick. By the time [Peter and Jane] reached Seguin, Texas, all four of the Pearson [children] were ill with diphtheria."[83]

Soon after their arrival in Seguin, the baby George, just short of three months, dies. Just six days later, Catherine Sarah Pearson, two, dies on September 24.

George and Sarah are buried in a cemetery in Seguin, Texas. "Peter Pearson was a skilled carpenter, and his first work in America was the building of the small coffins in which his two children were buried."[84]

Jane's sister, Mary, writes to her on October 28:

> We just think if we could have been with you to have shared your grief when the blow first fell upon you. But oh, my dear Sister there is a comforter, whose love is above all others & our earnest prayer is that he may pour his balm of consolation upon your poor wounded hearts.[86]

"Seguin was not the promised land after all. There was little there for Peter Pearson's highly skilled abilities. Jane worked as a skillful nurse—and her reputation was so widely recognized that the governor of Texas, Oran M. Roberts, asked her to care for his mother through a serious illness."[85]

1885 Jane gives birth to their fifth child. James Peter Pearson is born on May 8, in Seguin, Texas. The Pearsons move to the Lockehill Community (Shavano), 15 miles north of San Antonio.

1886 It must have been important for Peter and Jane to have their children well educated. When the oldest, Jennie, is 10, she stays with the Northcroft family in La Vernia, Texas, and attends school there. Jennie writes home to her mother on October 25:

> They are all kind to me...[Are] the three little chicks still living yet? .... Mr. Northcroft got me a third reader and a copy book and some nice pens and a good big slate and 6 slate pencils and he's teaching me now....[87]

1889 Jennie, now 13, attends the German-English School in San Antonio where she is in the 6th grade. Many years later, Jennie will tease her German husband, Almond, telling him that she knows German, too. And she'll recite the one sentence she learned at the German-English school. 'Der Schuhmacher macht Schuhe.' (The shoemaker makes shoes.)"[88]

1889 Peter and Jane's sixth child, William (Willie) Pearson, is born on October 12, in Bexar County, Texas, where Lockehill (Shavano) is located.

1895 Peter and Jane's seventh child, David Durward Pearson, is born on March 29, in Bexar County, Texas.

1898 Jane's mother Jane Sparks Durward whom she has not seen in 17 years, dies at the age of 79. Jane's sisters, Margaret (Maggie) Durward and Sarah Durward Eaton, immediately write Jane with the news. Sarah writes:

> No one was with her at the very last but Lizzie

230

Freeman and Maggie, father had just been a wee bit down the road . . . the end came quite suddenly. Some little time before, she stretched out her hands & said to Jesus to lead her kindly on, so he led her into his presence to be with him for evermore. On Saturday night —between 8 and 9 o'clock on the 12th of March, her spirit fled.

Lizzie Freeman and Maggie laid her in her winding shawl & with much love and tenderness performed the last-deed services to our beloved dead.[89]

1899 Jennie is now 22 and providing income for her family. She's been living in New Orleans working as a governess for the Scudder family. She develops a strong bond with Mrs. Scudder, but Jennie soon returns to Texas because of the danger of yellow fever in New Orleans.

Soon after Jennie returns from New Orleans, Almond Knolle notices her at the Lockehill Methodist Church. Years later Jennie will tell her daughter Mary, "I learned later that he had told his cousin, Willie Gehrels, that I was going to be his girl."[90]

1900 Jennie and Almond are in love and writing each other every day.

Almond asks Peter for Jennie's hand in marriage. He responds to Almond's request with wry humor, "It does not matter what I have to say, you will take her away from me regardless."[91]

Jennie and Almond marry on Thursday, September 20, 1900, at the home of Jennie's parents in Shavano. They will live in the little house Almond has built for her near Shavano and his bees on the

Donaldson place.

1907 Jennie and Almond buy 405 acres of land near Sandia, Texas.

1908 Jane and Peter move to Sandia, Texas to be near Jennie and Almond, who will soon follow with their first four children. Four more children will be born to Jennie and Almond and they will live together on their farm in Sandia for the next 61 years.

1920 Peter Pearson dies on September 18, 1920, at age 79 and is buried in the Lockehill Cemetery northwest of San Antonio.
The death of their two children so soon after they arrived in Seguin seemed to rob [Peter] of ambition since he came to feel his move to the United States had caused their death."[92]

1920 to 1935 Jane Pearson lives her later years at the homes of two daughters, Jennie Knolle and Maggie Schmid, and at the home of their son James and his wife Viola. Viola will affectionately report that Jane is "a terrible cook. When Jane burns the oatmeal cookies, she'll say, 'They're not burnt, they're just well done.'"[93]

1935 Jane dies on Feb 1, 1935, at Thelma, Bexar County. She is 85. She's buried next to Peter.
❖

The children of Peter and Jane Pearson didn't have easy lives. Jennie worked from an early age, and after marriage to Almond, she gave birth to eight children, raising them in a time of no plumbing or electricity. She never lost interest in the wider world she had left as a young girl, and somehow she managed to find time to correspond extensively with family members. Jennie often quoted from *The Keys of the Kingdom*, by the Scottish novelist and physician, A.J. Cronin, "There are many gates to heaven..." and she welcomed her ecumenical family with generosity and hospitality.

Fig. 76 Maggie Pearson Schmid

Maggie Pearson Schmid is said to have "had an abiding love for her Scotch heritage, . . . her life was not easy since times were hard and money scarce, and [her husband] Sam's restless nature fostered much moving from one place to another. Maggie was artistic and musical and had a keen intelligence, deep perception and the courage to speak her convictions."[94] She died December 3, 1958, at age 78, in Corpus Christi, and is buried in the Lockehill Cemetery near her parents.

James Pearson became a skilled carpenter. He and his wife Viola made their home in Banquete, Texas. He died in 1961 at the age of 75. Years later, Mary Margaret Knolle would write her poem, "James, the Carpenter:"

"It's just whatever a person wants."
Often he said this
With cheerful acceptance
As he constructed
A house or a cow-pen,
Faithfully following
The plans of other men
While gently postponing
Dreams of his own.[95]

William (Willie) Pearson moved to Sandia in 1907, and he lived there his entire life. He remained a bachelor and died in 1980, at the age of 91. The Reverend James Mayfield began the eulogy: "I understand that at one time Willie had the honor and responsibility of keeping the pick and shovel for the cemetery. It is a good symbol, this pick and shovel, of the way he cared. He cared in terms of deeds, not words or merely feelings.[96]"

Peter and Jane's youngest child, David Pearson was jovial and popular. After his parents moved to Sandia in 1908, he went to the Sandia school. In World War I, he kept a colorful and fast-moving diary, but he never fully recovered from being gassed in France. His nephew, Henry Knolle, would later write:

After the war ended and David did get home,

there were several other Sandia boys who returned about the same time, and there was much rejoicing and celebrating . . . The social activity in Sandia really came to life with at least two or three parties a week and sometimes a dance at night. There were fish fries and community-wide picnics down on the river . . . David was always at the front of these affairs.[97]

David's wife Irene Evans died just six years after their marriage. He died in 1960, age 65, at the Veterans Hospital in Kerrville, Texas, and is buried with Irene near their home in Spicewood, Texas.[98]

Jane Pearson never returned to her "ain countrie," but she carried with her values from there that enabled her to cope with her difficult life. Her Calvinistic upbringing helped her accept the death of her babies in a new land, and it enabled her to rise above humiliating circumstances. She was injured when she was kicked in the back by a cow. She picked cotton, and she never had a home of her own. She accepted hard work with dignity, and her lack of bitterness and her faith is remembered by her family through generations.

Peter, too, accepted his lot in life with perseverance. Death, injury, and rough Texas life robbed him of his youthful promise and ambition He kept his sense of humor in spite of depression and discouragement. At the end of his life, Peter delighted in the great affection of his grandson Durward.

Without intending to, Jane and Peter modeled courage and constancy in the face of hardship.

James Pearson(1807-1876) m. Elizabeth Birrell (1807-1860)	David Durward(1818-1903) m. Jane Sparks(1819-1898)

Peter Pearson Family

Peter Pearson (1841-1920)
m.
Jane Durward (1855-1935)

Jennie (1876-1972) m. Almond Knolle	Margaret (1878-1958) m. Sam Schmid
Sarah (1879-1881) died at 2 yrs.	George (1881) died at 3 months
James (1885-1961) m. Viola Bode	David (1895-1960) m. Irene Evans
Willie (1889-1967)	

Peter Pearson was one of 5 children. Jane Durward was one of 11 children.

Katie (2) and George (3 mos) died of diphtheria within days after the family arrived in Seguin, TX, 1881.

Willie remained a bachelor all of his life.

Appendix 3: The Land

The Casa Blanca Land Grant (1798-1908)

When Almond and Jennie Knolle bought land on the Lower Nueces River in 1907, they probably didn't know that the land was part of the original Casa Blanca Land Grant which had seen Spanish explorers come through around 1521.

By 1907 Almond and Jennie had three children with a fourth on the way. When Henry, the first boy, was born in 1906, Almond began planning to buy land for him. Almond was 31 by then, and his friends were full of "land fever."[99] Almond was shrewd and looked around first with his friend Mr. Adair, who'd bought 1,110 acres near Dinero, Texas.

Almond went home to talk to Jennie. They must have made the decision with great thought because Almond waited for six months before he went back. Many years later, he described that second trip:

> Around Thanksgiving in 1906, I came down again, this time on the train. I looked at land along the Nueces River and then looked at this where we live [now]. I went back to the river where people were buying land because it was fairly clear with little expense of grubbing. But I came back and bought these 405 acres from Mr. Dibrell for $20.00 an acre. I bought it because it had heavy timber. I just figured it must be good land to grow such big mesquite trees.[100]

Within a few years, Almond and Jennie had made their home on those 405 acres, and through exhausting hard work, they'd created a good living for themselves and their eight children.

Almond and Jennie's land is sitting on the old Casa Blanca Land Grant of Juan José de la Garza Montemayor. Its territory had been inhabited for at least 11,000 years by indigenous peoples of South Texas.[101]

The Casa Blanca Land Grant is bordered by the oldest natural ford on the Lower Nueces River and "had been used since earliest times by buffalo, Indians, explorers, soldiers, freighters, stages, and travelers."[102] On the right bank of the river just across the ford, archaeologists excavating "at Round Lake date an Indian Presence in the area as far back as about A.D. 1400."[103]

1689 About this time, the ford becomes known as the Paso de Margarita [Margarita Crossing] on El Camino Real de la Tejas [The Old San Antonio Road]. El Camino Real is established by Spanish explorers as they come from the southern Rio Grande to the Paso de Santa Margarita and on to East Texas to set up colonies and missions.[104]

1754 The Casa Blanca Fort is built by Tomás Sánchez de la Barrera y Gallardo, captain of Laredo. "The Casa Blanca (the White House) is constructed of caliche blocks known as ciares. The house is built in the shape of a square with a courtyard in the center. The well in the courtyard also serves as the entrance to a tunnel out of the building."[105]

The site is difficult to defend from constant Indian raids and attacks by bands of outlaws, and the settlement is soon abandoned.

1780's Spanish priests try to create at Casa Blanca a "kind of sub-mission attached to the La Bahia and Goliad [missions]." But the priests soon abandon Casa Blanca as well.[106]

The legends of buried treasure at Casa Blanca begin with this sub-mission. Texas historian J. Frank Dobie explains that all sorts of stories ascribing treasure to the 'mission' . . . were told, and they are yet believed."[107]

1798 Juan José de la Garza Montemayor makes the first payment for Casa Blanca Land Grant [originally the Penitas Grant], and the Spanish crown sends a surveying party to assess the land. The grant consists of 70,000 acres or 16 Spanish leagues, sitios, between Penitas Creek and the Nueces River.[108]

The surveying team finds the land to contain "an abundance of wolves, coyotes, and snakes, a shortage of water, and a vulnerability to attacks by the barbaric Indians The land was therefore evaluated at a mere ten pesos per league."[109]

1805 In February, the Spanish crown officially grants the Casa Blanca land to Juan José de la Garza Montemayor and his sons, José Manuel, Perfecto, and Agustin.[110]

1807 The Montemayors establish a ranch close to Penitas Creek. Since it's near the site of Casa Blanca Fort, the ranch is called Casa Blanca.

Fig. 77 Section of May 1896 map of Nueces County Texas, including the Gulf Coast Region

1816 Juan José de la Garza Montemayor dies, and legends of buried treasure multiply. People at the time were pretty certain that the ranch was generating vast wealth.

J. Frank Dobie recounts, "By 1810, according to a dubious source, the Garza Montemayors numbered their herds at 60,000 sheep, 24,000 cattle, and 14,000 horses; but in that year, Indians overpowered them and razed the walls of their stronghold."[111] Did Garza Montemayor die in that Indian raid?

Another version, Dobie writes that "old Montemayor, the ranchero of Casa Blanca, at length

240

sold out his vast herds, acquiring hard cash in payment. He was preparing to transport it and his family to a more civilized place when some Mexican bandits . . . captured him and tortured him until he told where the cash was hidden. . . Then they killed him."[112] Was the old ranchero killed by the bandits?

Even more violence is connected to this version of the story. It seems that the first bandits found out that a second group of bandits was spying on them. The first bandits "under cover of night . . . hid their booty in a rock pen adjacent to the Casa Blanca stronghold, burying the body of the murdered ranchero on top of it so that his spirit would act as patron, or guard.

"The two groups of bandits fight; the first bandits are killed, but one of the victorious bandits learns the treasure's location. He is shot and killed as he tries to make it to the Rio Grande.[113]

1825 Near Casa Blanca on the west bank of the Nueces River, Fort Lipantitlan is established by José Maria J. Carbajal to restrict Anglo immigration to Texas. The fort is named for the Lipan Apache Indians, who historically used the site as a campground. An old presidio built on this site as early as 1734 is a sign of the early existence of a Spanish military presence.[114]

1830 On the east bank of the Nueces near Fort Lipantitlan, John McMullen and James McGloin establish the Catholic colony of San Patricio de Hibernia.[115]

1835 As a part of the Texas Revolution, the Battle of Lipantitlan is fought along the Nueces River on November 4. The success of the Texians in this battle contributes to the eventual defeat of the Mexicans.

1840's The Mexican War (1846-48) brings General Zachary Taylor of the U.S. Army to Corpus Christi. A regular line of wagons begins transporting goods from Corpus Christi through San Patricio to San Antonio. San Patricio is not only near the Margarita Crossing and the Old San Antonio Road but is right over the Nueces from the Casa Blanca lands.[116]

J. Frank Dobie explains that around the same time "in the forties, Casa Blanca became, on account of the grassy prairies around and abundant water, a kind of rehabilitation headquarters for the great trains of Chihuahua carts freighting between Corpus and points in northern Mexico."[117]

1849 Juan Jose de la Garza Montemayor's widow, Josefa López de Jaen (Xaen) has retained Casa Blanca Ranch since Garza Montemayor's death in 1816. Now, she and their three sons sell much of the land to William Mann, a merchant, and trader from Corpus Christi.[118] He takes over the ranch and calls it the Mann Rancho. Already in 1848, he'd arranged an excursion to Casa Blanca to show investors the richness of the land. "From [La Casa Blanca] down to San Patricio, there is not a foot of land between the ridge and river that would not be called first rate." He will keep at least 26,000 acres for himself and divide the rest into parcels to sell to area farmers and ranchers.[119]

Mann and Henry Lawrence Kinney,[120] a land speculator and trader like Mann, organize the "Goodwill Merchandising Trip to Chihuahua." They want to reestablish the lucrative trade relationship between Chihuahua, Mexico, and Corpus Christi. Casa Blanca is the meeting point, and "hundreds of oxcarts packed to the brim arrive at Casa Blanca, widely known for its water supplies and abundant grasslands."

1862-1865 During the Civil War, at the ruins of the old Casa Blanca Fort, a Confederate post is established. The post is "supplied by small boats that outmaneuvered Federals on Nueces Bay, slipped into the Nueces River, and came up Penitas Creek."[121]

Those loyal to the Confederate cause "hauled guns, ammunition, medicine, and other wartime goods and took out cotton, 'Currency of the Confederacy.'"[122]

Finally, the wars of Spain, Mexico, and the Republic of Texas are over, and the Civil War is in the past. Fort Casa Blanca and nearby Fort Lipantitlan are in ruins. The Santa Margarita Crossing, the Camino Real, and the Old San Antonio Road are forgotten.

The wars have not destroyed the Casa Blanca lands. Abundant food sources remain. Watering holes, natural springs, and creeks provide a steady supply of water for the large sheep and cattle ranches to come.

1876 John Wade purchases 26,000 acres of Casa Blanca and moves his family into a small house on the ranch about two miles from the old Spanish Fort. John Wade's land will be called Wade's Rancho.

John Wade and his family settle on the "ranch in 1876, their first home being built with lumber shipped in from Florida by boat, being hauled to the present ranch by ox cart, where the present home now stands."[123]

1883 John Wade is only one of the early settlers who has bought tracts of land from William Mann. A survey in this year names many of them: Nicholas Bluntzer, Henry Redman, Richard King, J. S. Elliff, John Gallagher, T.C and Calvin Wright.

Bluntzer and Elliff and Gallagher have purchased adjoining tracts and have continual disputes about the boundaries of their land. Each had been setting up fences according to their ideas of where their land begins or ends. Surveyors are called in to settle the many disputes, and they re-survey the lines and re-establish the legal boundaries.

The main surveyor, A. M. French, must be a patient man. He records in the survey of Dec. 5, 1912, "Ever since these fences were built . . . the several owners have held adverse, open and notorious and peaceful possession of said land; that is Messrs. Elliff, Bluntzer, and Gallagher."[124]

1896 John Wade is ambitious and wants more than just the Wade Ranch. He develops his own town, and "because Casa Blanca [is] already established as a stopping point [he] establishes Wade City adjacent to it, platting streets and setting aside land for stores and churches. . . . In 1896 Casa Blanca-Wade City [has] a combined estimated population of 150, a Methodist church, a general store, a gin, and a lumberyard."[125]

1898 John Wade dies of a gunshot wound he received three years before during an attempted murder. Family stories passed down maintain that a disgruntled heir was responsible.[126]

Wade's Last Will and Testament divides the Wade Ranch and his other assets between his sons, John L. and Wallis Wade, and his three daughters, Sarah McNeill, Gertrude Wade, and Rosalind Newberry. Wallis inherits the bulk of the Wade Ranch. John L. Wade will later sell his inheritance of 9,000 acres to Joseph Burton Dibrell of Seguin, Texas.[127]

1907 Joseph Dibrell is a successful lawyer in

nearby Seguin. He gives "the task of dividing and selling the land to his son, Fennell Dibrell, and Max Starke who establish Sandia in 1907."[128]

"At the time the streets were platted there was only one building in the community. Dibrell and Starke chose the name Sandia, Spanish for "watermelon" because of the large number of watermelons grown in the area."[129]

Fig. 78 Section of 1920 Texas State map #10749
In the upper left corner, the towns of La Fruta, Sandia, Casa Blanca, San Patricio, and Bluntzer can be seen.

"The lots in Sandia were all sold within eight months, during which time a lumberyard, a hardware store, two grocery stores, a meat market, a boardinghouse, and a barbershop opened." A major draw for the new residents of Sandia is "a stop on the Texas and New Orleans Railroad."[130]

1907 Almond Knolle buys 405 acres of land two miles east of the new town of Sandia, He pays Joseph Dibrell $1500 down with a note for $8078 at 6% interest.

Almond and Jennie will live on those 405 acres for the rest of their lives.[131] Their children and grandchildren and great-grandchildren will refer to the 405 acres as the Home Place.

Fifty Years of Milking Jerseys
Knolle Jersey Farms 1928-1978

Almond Knolle was a young boy living in San Antonio in the late 1800's. He helped his widowed mother milk their few Jerseys and would deliver butter to the neighbors. Later, when he moved his own young family to Sandia, he kept a few Jersey cows on the Knolle farm. The rich milk the Jerseys produced was shipped to a creamery in San Antonio for the manufacture of butter. However, the severe drought of 1917 necessitated the sale of Almond Knolle's Jerseys.

But it was Almond's optimistic perseverance that was the cornerstone of strength in another endeavor which began in 1928. Almond and his oldest son, Henry, purchased 13 head of grade Jerseys. In 1931 Ed Knolle joined his father and his brother in the partnership of Knolle Jersey Farms. One of the first things they did was purchase a Sears & Roebuck milking machine. With the use of artificial insemination and two great bulls, Masterman Golden Jolly and Jester Aim, the 13 Jerseys evolved into the World's Largest Jersey Herd.

Beginning in 1938, Knolle Jerseys accumulated numerous national honors in the major show rings and over 2,000 official Jersey milk production records. Knolle bulls were sold and shipped throughout the world for breeding stock. In 1945 the formation of Knolle Jersey Milk Products provided for the distribution of dairy products throughout the Coastal Bend.

At its peak, Knolle Jersey Farms consisted of 13,000 acres of land in Nueces and Jim Wells counties and more than 8,000 registered Jerseys.

247

1928   Almond Knolle, 55, and his son, Henry, 22, purchase 13 head of grade Jersey cows from C.W. Vandiver in Alice, Texas.

1931 Edward Knolle, 19, joins Henry and their father, Almond, forming the partnership of Knolle Jersey Farms.

1936 Walton Knolle joins Knolle Jersey Farms, followed by Bob Knolle, both contributing to its rapid development.
The Knolle partnership purchases its first Jerseys registered by the American Jersey Cattle Club.
Late 1930s Paul Crisp is employed, establishing a long relationship between the Crisp family and the Knolles.

1939   Ed designs the first truck with a milk thermos tank which can be used for hauling 1600 gallons of milk. He has it made at the Heil Company in Milwaukee, Wisconsin. Before this time, dairy farmers transported the milk in 2 to 3-gallon milk cans.

1940   Henry and Ed buy the Taft Ranch Jersey herd from B. H. Cummins. Cummins had been manager of the Taft Ranch Jerseys for many years and had purchased the herd upon retirement. In this group of Jerseys is Masterman Golden Jolly, who will become the major herd sire of Knolle Jersey Farms.

1941   Henry and Ed drive to Ontario and acquire a one-year-old bull Jester Aim from the well-known Canadian Jersey herd of B. H. Bull & Son. Jester Aim will become a second major herd sire at Knolle Jersey Farms and will be bred to daughters of

Masterman Golden Jolly.

1943 Knolle Jersey Farms holds its first herd classification in April of this year. Official judges from the American Jersey Cattle Club grade 40 Knolle Jerseys. Four hundred people attend a barbecue and celebrate the event. These 40 Jerseys are the first of many thousands of Knolle Jerseys to be officially classified throughout the years.

1945 Knolle Jersey Milk Products plant opens in Corpus Christi. The first milk is processed, packaged, and offered for sale in the early part of February of this year.

1948 Arthur Knolle joins the family enterprise after a successful career as a pioneer aviator. Arthur loves flying, but he also has an inherent love for farming. He and Ed plant the first Coastal Bermuda grass on the Farm which is the beginning of the green sea of permanent grass, which now covers Knolle Jersey Farms and other Coastal Bend pastures.

In this year, Masterman Golden Jolly dies. *The Corpus Christi Caller-Times* runs a feature story: "The Masterman is dead. But his memory will remain alive as long as the Jersey breed exists; for the breed and Masterman Golden Jolly have become synonymous."[132]

1950s The Farms expand steadily and have to overcome blows such as the severe drought of the '50's when the adaptable Jersey have to survive on mesquite and hackberry leaves, prickly pear, and imported feed.[133]

1952 Knolle Jersey Farms has become "The

World's Largest Jersey Herd."[134] The Farms consists of 13,000-acres of land in Nueces and Jim Wells counties and 3000 head of purebred Jerseys; 1450 Jersey cows are being milked twice daily; 4027 Jerseys owned by the Farms have been officially classified by the American Jersey Cattle Club, and 50% of the Jersey cattle are now bred artificially.[135]

By this year, 150 employees and their families live on the Farms where 7000 acres are farmed for feed for the Jerseys. Eight trench silos hold 20,000 tons of feed. It takes eight ensilage cutters, six large dump trucks, 30 tractors, and 32 cars and trucks to get the Farms' work done.[136]

The Knolles decide to emphasize the quality of their show herd and hire Reginald Buesnel, a well-respected showman from the Island of Jersey. The French-speaking Buesnels move to the Farm with their three youngest children, Ron, Thelma, and Wayne.[137]

1958 More honors are awarded to Knolle Jersey Farms. Masterman Golden Jolly and Jester Aim are recognized in this year by the American Jersey Cattle Club as two of the five Century Sires of the breed.[138]

1959 The growth of the Farms leads to the construction of a new office which triples the workplace. Trophy cases are built, and a visitor's area is created for interested dairymen and busloads of school children.

Knolle cousins Ginny, Louise, Pearson, and Charles win the state 4-H Dairy Judging Contest and travel to Waterloo, Iowa, to represent the state of Texas. They compete against college teams and place 5th in Jersey judging.

Fig. 79 Texas Dairy Judging Team travels to Iowa for national competition, 1959 . Team coach, Charles Neal. From top to bottom, Ginny, Louise, Pearson, and Charles

1960 Texas Governor John Connally appoints Edward Knolle to the Texas Animal Health Commission. Ed will be reappointed to the commission by four governors—John Connally, Preston Smith, Dolph Briscoe, and Bill Clements.

Ed serves on the commission for 18 years and as chairman for 5 years.[139] At his retirement in 1987, he will be given a plaque inscribed with words written by his friend J.W. Sartwelle with whom he served:

Presented with sincere respect and appreciation to
C.E. "Ed" Knolle who represented the dairy industry on the
Commission. A man of gracious character and good humor
and one who provided distinctive leadership and dedicated
service to the livestock industry of Texas,
Texas Animal Health Commission
Austin, Texas [140]

1961 The annual meeting of the American
Jersey Cattle Club is held in Corpus Christi with the
Knolle family hosting the event. Six-hundred Jersey
breeders from all over the world tour the Farm, view
the Jerseys, and picnic at the River Park.[141]

Ed is awarded the American Jersey Cattle
Club's Master Breeder Award for "having made a
notable contribution to the advancement of the Jersey
breed in the United States."[142] Thirty years later in
1991, Henry will also receive the award for Master
Breeder, making Ed and Henry the only two brothers
to have ever been individually named Master
Breeder.[143]

In this same year, Louise Knolle is named
American Dairy Princess in September in Chicago,
Illinois. She leaves her classes at SMU and travels for a
year in the United States, Canada, and South America,
representing the American Dairy Association.[144]
Louise speaks to school children, dairymen, and
legislators. She opens cattle expositions, meets with
livestock officials, and also milks cows in hotel lobbies.

This year also brings the highlight of Knolle
show ring honors when Mike's Draconis Rose owned
by Joe Knolle is named Grand Champion Jersey cow
at the All-American Jersey Show.[145]

1965 The Knolle bull Golden Etta Commando

sells for $22,500, the highest price ever recorded in any All-American Jersey Sale to this date.[146]

1967 Henry receives the Distinguished Service award, making him one of only four individuals to receive both the Master Breeder and the Distinguished Service awards of the American Jersey Cattle Club.[147]

1968 The Gulf Coast Chapter of the Boy Scouts of America presents a bronze trophy to the Knolles. The trophy commemorates the 20th year of the annual Boy Scout camporee at Knolle Jersey Farms River Park on the Nueces River under a forest of 1500 year old Live Oak trees. An estimated total of 60,000 Boy Scouts have camped for 23 consecutive years.[148]

The River Park has been maintained for the use of the general public for over 25 years by Knolle Jersey Farms. Uncounted thousands visit the Farms, and nearly every nation is represented in the office guest register.

1969 Almond Knolle dies on July 22, at the age of 94. Hours before he dies, his daughter Ruth whispers to him that man has walked on the moon.

1970 Hurricane Celia hits the Coastal Bend in August, and its damage is even more devastating 30 miles inland than it is on the coast. Celia leaves Knolle Jersey Farms without electricity for two weeks. With 4000 cows needing to be milked twice a day, this is an overwhelming loss.

1970-1980 More devastating than natural disasters are those imposed by man. Fifty years of government attempts at eradication of brucellosis forces the slaughter of thousands of registered Jerseys at a tremendous cost to the Farm.

Ed Knolle, a member and former chairman of the Texas Animal Health Commission, works unceasingly for the control of brucellosis in all breeds of cattle.

1971 Knolle Jersey Milk Products merges with Hygeia Dairy Company. At the time of the merger, there are 175 employees at Knolle Jersey Milk Products in Corpus Christi.

1972 South Texas is embroiled in a controversy involving the site of a proposed dam. South Texas for Choke Canyon, a group led by Louise Knolle Schimmel, presents a petition with 32,000 signatures to the Texas Water Rights Commission. The hearing on the Nueces River Project is in Austin, Texas. The Commission recommends the Choke Canyon site.

Henry and Ed Knolle dissolve Knolle Jersey Farms partnership and partition their land. Over 225 employees are working on the Farm at this time. Ed and Henry amicably divide their holdings, and each continues to run his individual family dairy operation.

1987 In his retirement, Ed begins a beef cow/calf operation. He invents a simple way of transplanting the little oak trees he's grown from acorns, and he plants thousands of oak trees on the Farm and the surrounding area. Governor Dolph Briscoe appoints Ed to a three-man Dairy Advisory Board, and he serves as a Councilor of the Texas A&M Research Foundation during the late 1980's.[149]

Henry Knolle serves on the board of Hygeia Dairy Company for the next 20 years. He develops his own herd of polled Jersey cattle for which he will be honored at the San Antonio Livestock Exposition in

1997.

Henry and Ed remain actively involved in working cattle and running their businesses well into their 90's. Henry's sons, Pearson and Joe, will continue milking Jersey cattle. Pearson's daughter, Karin, and Joe's son Joe Knolle, Jr. will continue the family tradition of supporting the Jersey industry and milking Jersey cattle.

1976 The Knolle Family is honored by Texas A&M University as a "Centennial Leader for Outstanding Contributions to Texas Agriculture during a Century of Change."[150]

Appendix 4: Poems by Mary Margaret Knolle

Vermillion Fly Catcher*

I plummet from the winter sky
To catch an unsuspecting fly.
I pause upon a rustic fence,
Quivering to recommence
My crimson aviary art.
Into the wind, I quickly start
Ascending to celestial air—
My grandiose theater where
I, the brown-masked thespian, jest
Mimicking the fabled quest
Of Icarus, the foolish one
Whose waxed wings melted in the sun,
And plunged him, scarlet as an ember,
Earthward to immortal splendor.

*a saucy little red bird with brown-
masked eyes
that winters in South Texas skies.

January 1980

The Guided Missile

This Tortuga on the sun-baked sand

Is warm as when it left the hand

Of an archaic hunter.

I rise to quell a primal fear

Of apparitions hovering near

To claim my plunder.

A shadow falls across the mound—

My own, now momentarily bound

In the dust of antiquity.

Where the missile, source unknown,

Wrought from stone with stone and bone,

Points toward infinity.

August 1976

L.M.B. (1897-1972)

I followed her gaze to the window
Where a white cloud graced the sky.
Her eyes, still eloquent,
 Escaped the sterile room
And sought the beautiful.
I knew that I would soon forget
Her years in an imprisoned body
And then remember only
Her light, quick step
As she walked through a mundane world.

July 1972

The Sorceress

When Jill was three
She said to me
As she lay on her back in the grass,
"Sometimes I like to think about God,"
She was watching a cloud drift past,
"And He looks like a handsome Prince."
Changed by the charm of innocence,
Michelangelo's gray God in the sky
Was suddenly young—and so was I.

1970

With Mrs. Columbus in Mind

Blue paint still tints the driveway
Where his paint can overturned
When he painted 'El Dorado'
On an ancient rowboat's stern.

It was the first of many crafts
He launched so happily
And with each boat he ventured
Farther out upon the sea.

———————————

My thoughts are on the waters
Of the Caribbean Sea
Where a hurricane is blowing
And a boat is on the lea—

A vessel, small but sturdy,
That has weathered storms before
And at its helm, a seaman
Who will bring it back to shore.

But it will be a long time
Ere I hear his tale
Of fireballs in the rigging
Or a wind that ripped a sail.

Because a sailor thinks that mothers
Should settle down like wine,
Undisturbed though brewing
Until the proper time.

September 1980

"Long ago …."

Long ago
I climbed the tall mulberry tree
In the big chicken yard
Where no one could find me
Which was about a mile from the kitchen.
And no one knew where I was
And I read forbidden books
And feasted on purple berries
And threw a few to the white leghorns
From my hidden library.
And I never answered when
They were looking for me And calling my name

Yesterday I went back
To the big silent house.
The mulberry tree which had
Grown very small
Was only a few yards from the kitchen window.
And anyone must have known where I was.
And the books were only Zane Grey
And the mulberries had ants in them.
And no one ever disturbed me or called me
Because they were enjoying the quiet peaceful house.

The Venerable Temperance Society of San Patricio de Hibernia

Ah, do you remember, James
The Temperance Society?
It was a handsome band they made
(Though very few in number)
When they dressed in Sunday best
And marched with fervor
To the Church
For the annual pledge
Of Temperance—
An admirable ambition for the Irish!
In the second year
The Grand March was scheduled
But no one came.

(As told to me in 1972 by
Robert Bluntzer.
This Grand March
occurred in the early
1870's.)

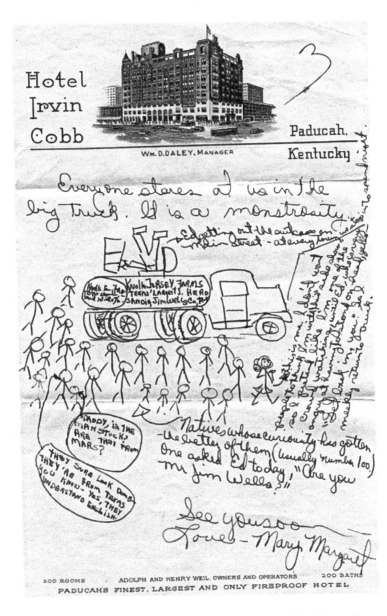

Drawing by Mary Margaret Knolle about her trip back from Milwaukee referenced in Fig 70, page 180

Where Did You Get That Hat?

Since nineteen hundred and six, I see
That hat has sat on top of thee!
When you were young the hat was wee:
It seemed to grow along with ye.
Where did you get that hat, Henry?
Gallantly lifting the hat from his head,
This is what Henry said:

"Napoleon wore it a time or two
During the Battle of Waterloo.
This I heard when I shook the hand
Of a man who shook hands
With a very old man
Who once shook the hand of Napoleon.
"Napoleon picked up the hat by chance
On the shore of the cold North Sea in France.
There it had drifted from Stonehaven, Scotland
Where the Durward-Pearson clan was begotten.

"Then in eighteen hundred and thirty-six,
Texas was in an awful fix.
But Sam Houston made no error
When he told his friend Bernard Scherrer,
'Rustle some beeves for my hungry men—
The San Jacinto battle is about to begin!
So, Scherrer was up the Brazos when,
With his Enfield rifle in his hand,
He shot this hat he wore from Switzerland—
Back in eighteen hundred and twenty nine!
I'm proud of that great grandpa of mine.
(His Enfield rifle was the kind that tends,
When shot, to get meat at both ends.)

264

"In eighteen hundred and forty four
This same hat Ernst Knolle wore
After he emigrated from Germany
To the Texas town of Industry.
That hat is pierced with a hole or two—
One a Comanche arrow went through,
And one from the War with Mexico—
Ernst sent his hat, but he couldn't go.
On the brim is the Battle of Vicksburg scar—
His son Hermann wore it to the Civil War.

"In nineteen eighteen, by grim circumstance,
Uncle David Pearson wore it to France.
My Papa found it necessary
To wear it in his apiary.
When I was young, he gave it to me,
The first of five sons in his family.
And I wear it very attractively."
(While Henry adjusted the hat on his head,
Florence remarked that he wears it in bed.)

Well, the hat's magnificent history
Is as clear as it will ever be—
The hat, the facts and a bit of folly
Are all from the head of Henry Knolle

Note: the facts are underlined

(This is exactly the way she wrote it, including the
underlining and the line at the end.)

265

Appendix 5:
Notes Aboard the *Fata Morgana*
by Charles Knolle

Maine – 1978

When three schooners, one right after the other, tacked into our cove and dropped anchor, I knew there must be something wrong. In these days one schooner is news, three in a bunch are almost unheard of. It was soon apparent that the vessels were dude-carriers. Their decks instead of being loaded with pulp wood held that most precious freight – men and women on excursion.

I dinghied out from the *Fata Morgana* to see the sights and was invited aboard one of the vessels by an enthusiastic young sea dog who, after three full days afloat, was bursting with information of a fervishly nautical character. He kept tying knots in things and rushed me all over the boat, above and below, showing off its rude appointments and instructing me in the proper handling of a schooner in fair weather and foul, including the management of a huge sail called, unexplained, the Jib-top Flap-sail.

The small yawls, equivalent of our dinghy, were busy taking passengers ashore for a lobster dinner on the beach, and our usually quiet anchorage, whose only regular night visitors had been me and a great blue heron, was soon busy with the urgent screams and cries of persons temporarily removed from their normal environment.

I was told that the schooners were all owned by one man – he has five or six of them and is buying others as fast as he can find them. Dude business is good. Not much has to be done with the ships – some bunks built into the hold, a toilet installed, a new sail or two, and some paint. They are old boats, most of them, but plenty good enough for summer–time cruising, and are completely sailed by Maine captains, who accept the arrivals of vacationers on their foredeck with the same stoical reserve with which they accept fog on a flood tide at evening.

The invasion of these beautiful Eastern schooners by paying guests who are not sailors is an American phenomenon I've grown used to. It's hard to say why the spectacle is saddening to the spirit, but there is no denying the way I feel when I see a coaster that has lost her legitimate deck load and acquired a crew of part-time gypsies. There is nothing wrong about it – anybody who is having a good time can't be wrong – yet the eternal quest for the romantic past that lives on in the minds of men and causes them to strike attitudes of hardihood in clothes that don't quite fit them is so often a quest for the unattainable. And it ends so abruptly in reality.

A Night Watch
Bahamas to St. Thomas, U.S.V.I.

We are in the cabin. Debbie is asleep across from my perch on the high side of the boat, which is staggering through rough seas and a 20-knot head wind. Debbie is protected from falling out of bed by the canvas leeboards. When the port side of the boat is the windward side and you are hewed over hard, as we have been for four days now, you need to extricate the lee straps from under your mattress. We placed them conveniently equipped with snap-hooks, so you only need to find the corresponding eyelets on the overhead and hook them in.

It has been an unsatisfactory day. The conditions of the course are hard, Debbie, simply put, is miserable. I am as usual silent, dwelling mentally on what next will go wrong. I'm reading a book about horses – never at sea do we read sea stories or Gothic-Romantic Novels.

Unsteady Debbie continues to work out my sight-reduction-observations. We're in agreement with our dead reckoning and far enough from the reefs and shoals of Bermuda to navigationally relax, except for odd-shaped container cargo ships and brilliantly lit cruise ships all on the offing and on, it seems, a collision course with the *Fata Morgana*. With my color-blindness, Debbie is called on deck to verify relative course and position. Navigation is no problem if weather is clear – if not – Bermuda and her surrounding reefs are a hazard.

Meals, in rough weather, are utilitarian: soup in bowls, bread and cheese and wine.

We pick up an A.M. frequency from the States, warning us to don galoshes and carry an umbrella.

Dawn is an hour away and the watch changes.

That means, on a doublehanded boat that you worry about yourself while on watch and then, off watch, you worry about your mate topside and can't sleep anyway.

And on it goes, until landfall, and you're so tired you don't want to go in. Stay in your home element and to hell with the flashing city lights.
[N]o time to finish this.

Appendix 6: Poems by Katherine Knolle Horrigan

South Texas Baptism

Algae-green the font
The tiny church
Humid as a fishmarket
The congregation
Uneasy and hot
Blessed Assurance 218
Chest high water
Preacher and Sinner
Eyes closed tight
An arm reaches up
Stretched toward heaven
With fingers apart
Wanting a piece of
The Great Teacher's time
"Almighty God"
The lady goes under
Waves lap against glass
Rising she gurgles and spits out "O Lordy"
God's audience waves
Popsicle stick fans
Fifty faces of Jesus
In auburn-haired bliss
Look on the reverse
For spiritual guidance
Dobie Funeral Home

Evolution

Then our heads were small and brown
Cave-painted with suns and moons
Now our heads are big and green
Printed, if you look closely,
With presidents' faces
In this darkness our eyes grow large
Looking further down the road
Where it won't be dark
Where we won't be lonely

Appendix 7:
A Trip in the Buggy with Papa
by Mary Knolle Sims

Mary Durward Knolle Sims, our "Aunt Mary D.," was the oldest of Jennie and Almond Knolle's eight children. She lived in Houston most of her life and taught English at Lamar High School for many years. I haven't written about Mary; she speaks for herself in this essay taken from a longer piece, "This Was Our Life as told to Mary Knolle Sims in 1960 by Jennie Pearson Knolle."

The excitement of those drives still lingers after more than fifty years. In a starched gingham dress and sunbonnet, long black wide-ribbed stockings, and high buttoned shoes, I sat beside Papa and waved to Mama as Jim started down the road. It thrilled me to know that in a few hours I would be out in those hazy blue hills among the guajillo. Passing corn and cotton fields, hay meadows and dairy farms, we headed toward the hills. Papa entertained me with stories about working in Wolff and Marx Dry Goods Store in San Antonio as a cash boy. Then he sang "Two Little Girls in Blue" and "Grandfather's Clock" until I became sleepy. Papa then sat forward on the buggy seat and straightened me out behind him, where I stretched full length. When I waked, we were in the hills driving over a rocky, halfmarked trail.

The air was crisp and fragrant with guajillo. Occasionally, a bright flash of white brush bloom broke the expanse of guajillo. A startled covey of quail took wing with a frightening roar. Papa lifted me out of the buggy and together we walked through the guajillo examining buds and blossoms. He broke off a twig of white brush for me, which I handled somewhat gingerly because of the thorns but couldn't resist because of the fragrance. The hum of the bees filled the air. I could sense Papa's mood of anticipation. "Bees are working," he said; "we'll have a good honeyflow in a couple of weeks." I always felt happy when Papa had a burst of financial enthusiasm, for even then I knew that he provided my bread and honey.

Another long drive brought us to the apiary and honey house, where Papa unhitched and fed Jim. Then we spread a camp blanket under a mesquite tree where we ate our lunch of fried chicken, deviled eggs, and homemade bread with butter and honey. From a little bucket Papa filled my tin cup with milk. What a good lunch, I thought, until ants swarmed over the blanket and into the bread and honey. I was amazed at Papa's utter disregard of this onslaught. Ignoring the ants, he ate sandwich after sandwich, assuring me that a few ants were good for a person. I really believed him, and with a new sophistication ate ants along with the bread and honey.

I sat in the buggy under a mesquite tree while Papa hoed around the beehives. He always kept them in straight rows with all the weeds cut. Then together we inspected the honey house...the big extractor tank with its swinging wire baskets, the wide uncapping knives, the wheelbarrows, and the smokers. Papa untied my bonnet and put his bee veil on my head. His old felt hat almost covered my eyes, but I tucked the cheesecloth under my collar and looked out through the wire screening. Under that felt hat and veil, I felt almost on par with Papa: I had learned to eat ants gracefully, and now I could face a swarm of bees.

Papa finally locked the honey house, hitched Jim, and lifted me into the buggy for our drive home. Before leaving the hills, we stopped to gather wildflowers for Mama. Patches of crimson wineglasses, pink phlox, and purple verbena spread before us. I couldn't resist breaking a few sprigs of horsemint for its pungent fragrance. We put the flowers in a honey bucket and poured water from the jug to keep them fresh. Almost dark, Papa took out his gun and killed some doves which he put in the back of the buggy.

Papa was always cheerful and optimistic, but life must have seemed especially good to him that day, for again he sang. Neither the tired horse plodding along the country road nor the small admiring daughter at his side offered any static, so he sang with all the enthusiasm of his thirty years. Captivated by Papa, I scarcely noticed that we had turned into our road and that Mama was standing at the back gate waiting for us.

END NOTES

Introduction to Part One: The Wade Ranch 1890s-1970's

1   Copy of Last Will and Testament of John Wade, Notice in Probate Dated June 13, 1898. Recorded: Vol. "H" p. 255-8 prob. Minutes N.C. No. 86 Estate of John Wade, deceased #625, 121- 123.

Appendix 1 The Owings, Masons, and Buchanans

The Owings and the Masons: Colonial Americans

2   Mary Alice Mason Dunlap, compiler, Mason Family History, 1983, Knolle Family Papers.

3   Block, W. T., "Thomas Deye Owings of Maryland, Kentucky, and Texas: Frontier Iron-Smelterer and Military Hero,"
http://www.wtblock.com/wtblockjr/ thomas_deye_owings.htm.

4 Samuel Smith (Maryland), https://en.wikipedia.org/wiki Samuel_Smith_(Maryland).

5 Nicholas Smith, 1659–18 November 1718, **https://ancestors.familysearch.org/en/ L5NK-G4T/nicholas-smith-1659-1718.**

6 Ibid.

7 Dunlap, compiler, Mason Family History.

8 S. F. Austin to T. D. Owings, John H. Jenkins (ed.), Papers of the Texas Revolution, 1835- 1836, vol. 4, 54-55.

9 E. L. Hawes, "Texas 'Annexation, Mexican War, Clay's Defeat," San Antonio Express, San Antonio, Texas, Sunday Morning, October 20, 1935, 1D.

10 Dunlap, compiler, Mason Family History.

11 Block, "Thomas Deye Owings."

12 Ibid.

13 Mason-Fassett, wedding announcement, Sentinel, Mt. Sterling, Kentucky, November 7, 1883.

14 Mary Margaret Knolle, notes from conversation with Jim Mason, San Antonio, 1976, Knolle Family Papers.

15 Knolle, notes from conversation with Jim Mason.

16 John Calvin Mason [Louise Mason's older brother] to Louise Mason, May 23, 1917, Knolle Family Papers.

Sanford and Pinkie Buchanan: To Texas from the Old South

17 Ellen Castelow, "The Battle of Pinkie Cleugh," **https://www.historic-uk.com/HistoryMagazine/DestinationsUK/The-Battle-of- Pinkie-Cleugh/.**

18 Sanford Buchanan, obituary, Corpus Christi Caller, Friday, June 23, 1972, Knolle Family Papers.

19 "Funeral Services Held Monday for Floyd Buchanan," [newspaper not recorded], June 27, 1942.

20 Mary Margaret Knolle, "Notes Buchanan," 1988, Knolle Family Papers.

21 "Funeral Services Held Monday for Floyd Buchanan."

22 Louise Mason Buchanan to Perkins & Floyd, Alice, Texas, July 17,1942.

23 Ibid.

24 Ibid.

25 Ibid.

26 Ibid.

Appendix 2: The Scherrers, Knolles, and Pearsons

Bernard Scherrer: Citizen of the Republic of Texas

27 Copy of Bernard Scherrer's Swiss passport issued at St. Gallen, Switzerland, November 19, 1829, Knolle Family Papers.

28 "Anna Margreta Scherrer," obituary, La Grange Journal, February 28, 1935, Fayette County Obituaries **http://www.fayettecountyhistory.org obituaries.htm.**

29 Detlef Dunt, Journey to Texas, 1833, transl. by Anders Saustrup, edited and with an Introduction by James C. Kearney and Geir Bentzen, reprint, Austin, University of Texas Press, 2017.

30 Copy of Bernard Scherrer's Republic of Mexico passport issued at Brazoria, April 29, 1833, Knolle Family Papers.

31 Julia [M.] Collins, "Bernard Scherrer," Knolle Family Papers.

32 Julia [M.] Collins, "Scherrer, Bernard," Handbook.

33 Collins, "Scherrer, Bernard," Handbook.

34 Julia [M.] Collins, "Bernard Scherrer," Knolle Family Papers.

35 Julia [M.] Collins, "Scherrer, Bernard," Handbook.

36 Collins, "Scherrer, Bernard," Handbook.

37 Julia [M.] Collins, "Bernard Scherrer," Knolle Family Papers.

38 Collins, "Bernard Scherrer," Knolle Family Papers.

39 Julia [M.] Collins, "Scherrer, Bernard," Handbook.

40 Mary Margaret Knolle, "Papa's First Home," conversation with Belle Gallagher and Katherine Knolle, June 1, 1975, Knolle Family Papers.

41 Wayne Gard, "Coxey's Army," Handbook, accessed November 19, 2020, **https:// www.tshaonline.org/handbook/entries/coxeys-army.**

42 "Geronimo in San Antonio," **https://www.texascooppower.com/texas-stories/history/geronimo-in-san-antonio.**

43 Mary Margaret Knolle, "Almond Henry Knolle," (1875 – 1969), Knolle Family Papers.

44 Mary Margaret Knolle, notes from conversation with Ruth Knolle Lain, November 10, 1974, Knolle Family Papers.

45 Katherine Knolle, "Grandmothers in Review," 1960, Knolle Family Papers.

46 Knolle, "Grandmothers."

47 Mary Margaret Knolle, "Almond Henry Knolle," (1875 – 1969), Knolle Family Papers.

48 Daphne Dalton Garett, "Biegel, TX," Handbook, accessed December 16, 2020, **http://www.tshaonline.org/handbook/entries/biegel-tx**

The Knolles: The Industrious Ones

49 Ernst G. Knolle, Colma, California to Katherine Knolle, Sandia, Texas, January 2, 1965. Knolle Family Papers.

50 Ernst G. Knolle, Colma, California to Katherine Knolle, Sandia, Texas, January 2, 1965. Knolle Family Papers.

51 Frank [Francis White Johnson], A History of Texas and Texans, vol. 3, Chicago and New York: American Historical Society, 1916: download available free from Google Books **https://books.googleusercontent.com**

52 James and Ann Lindemann, "Industry, TX," Handbook, accessed November 20, 2020, **http://www.tshaonline.org/handbook/entries/industry-tx.**

53 Lindemann, "Industry, TX."

54 Johnson, A History of Texas and Texans, 1465.

55 Johnson, A History of Texas and Texans, 1465.

56 Sadie Mae Knolle Miller, compiler, A Collection of Historical Data on the Knolle Family, with a section on Ernst Hermann Knolle including his Civil War Diary, 49-96, Knolle Family Papers.

57 Miller, compiler, A Collection.

58 Miller, compiler, A Collection.

59 Miller, compiler, A Collection.

60 Miller, compiler, A Collection.

61 E. F. G. Knolle, Industry, Texas, to his brother, Johann Heinrich, Stadhagen, Germany, May 30, 1874, Knolle Family Papers.

62 E. F. G. Knolle, Industry, Texas, to his brother, Johann Heinrich, Stadhagen, Germany, May 30, 1874, Knolle Family Papers.

63 Mary Margaret Knolle, "Almond Henry Knolle," (1875 – 1969), Knolle Family Papers.

64 Mary Knolle Sims, "This Was Our Life" as told to Mary Knolle Sims in 1960 by Jennie Pearson Knolle, Knolle Family Papers.

65 F. M. Hicks to A.H. Knolle, Sandia, San Antonio, July 7, 1913. Knolle Family Papers.

The Pearsons: To Texas from Scotland by way of India

66 Letter of Reference for Peter Pearson from Daniel Craig, Brechin, [Scotland], October 3, 1859, Knolle Family Papers.

67 Letter of Reference for Peter Pearson from Adam Mitching, minister, Fettercairn, [Scotland], June 16, 1866, Knolle Family Papers.

68 Letter of Reference for Peter Pearson from Chas. Buril, farmer, Dallaris by Edzell, [Scotland], January. 16, 1866, Knolle Family Papers.

69 Mary Margaret Knolle, "Peter Pearson," [no date], Knolle Family Papers.

70 "Memorandum of Agreement" between Mess. Kirkpatrick and Martin and Peter Pearson," April 1, 1870, Knolle Family Papers.

71 "Coorg: The Scotland of India," **https://www.holidify.com/pages/scotland-ofindia-4222.html.**

72 Mary Margaret Knolle, "Notes on Peter Pearson Family from Records in Possession of Edward and Mary Margaret Knolle, Sandia, Texas," July 1974. Knolle Family Papers.

73 Knolle, "Notes on Peter Pearson Family."

74 Mary Margaret Knolle, notes on back of Peter and Jane Durward Pearson's wedding portrait, Knolle Family Papers.

75 Knolle, "Notes on Peter Pearson Family."

76 Scots in the American West,1783-1883 [database on-line]. Provo, UT, USA: Ancestry.com Operations Inc, 2006, original source: David Dobson, Scots in the American West, 1783-1883, Baltimore, MD, USA: Genealogical Publishing Co., 2003.**https://collectiowww.ancestry.com/search/cns /49337**

77 Knolle, "Notes on Peter Pearson Family."

78 Ruth Knolle Lain, notes from conversation in 1974 with Catherine Pearson, wife of Durward Pearson, from the Pearson's 1973 trip to Scotland, Knolle Family Papers.

79 Mary Margaret Knolle, notes compiled from conversations with Jennie Pearson Knolle about the Pearson's immigration experiences, September 9, 1981, Knolle Family Papers.

80 Louise Pettigrove's conversation with Carolyn Knolle about Carolyn's memories of Jennie Pearson Knolle's immigration stories, Summer 2020, Knolle Family Papers.

81 Lain, notes from conversation in 1974.

82 Knolle, notes compiled from conversations with Jennie Pearson Knolle.

83 Knolle, "Notes on Peter Pearson Family."

84 Knolle, "Notes on Peter Pearson Family."

85 Knolle, "Peter Pearson," [no date], Knolle Family Papers.

86 Mary Durward, Drumhendry, Lawrencekirk, Scotland to Jane Pearson, Seguin, October 28, 1881, Knolle Family Papers.

87 Jennie Pearson, La Vernia, Texas, to Jane Pearson, Lockehill [Shavano], Texas, October 25, 1886, Knolle Family Papers.

88 Mary Margaret Knolle, notes from conversation with Katherine Knolle, December 26, 1975.

89 Sarah Durward Eaton, Craig, Aberdeenshire, Scotland to Jane Durward Pearson, Lockehill, Texas, March 20, 1898.

90 Mary Knolle Sims, "This Was Our Life" as told to Mary Knolle Sims in 1960 by Jennie Pearson Knolle, Knolle Family Papers.

91 Mary Margaret Knolle, notes, September 9, 1981, Knolle Family Papers.

92 Knolle, "Notes on Peter Pearson Family."

93 Lain, notes from conversation in 1974.

94 Back of Photograph, Margaret (Maggie) Pearson Schmid, Knolle Family Photo Collection.

95 Mary Margaret Knolle, "James, the Carpenter (James Pearson)," "Other Poems," Poems and Plays, compiled by Louise Knolle Pettigrove, Knolle Family Papers.

96 Reverend James L. Mayfield, First Methodist Church, Mathis, Texas, "Mr. Pearson's Funeral [William "Willie" Pearson], Psalm 90, John 14:1-7, 15-17, 27, Monday, September 11, 1967.

97 Pearson, Henry Pearson, preface to David Pearson's WWI diary.

98 Ibid.

Appendix 3: The Land

The Casa Blanca Land Grant 1798-1908

99 Mary Knolle Sims, "'This Was Our Life 'as told to Mary Knolle Sims in 1960 by Jennie Pearson Knolle," Knolle Family Papers.

100 Sims, "'This Was Our Life'."

101 Native American Peoples of South Texas, edited by Bobbie L. Lovett, Juan L. González, Roseann Bacha-Garza Russell, K. Skowronek, The University of Texas – Pan American, Edinburg, Texas: Community Historical Archaeology Project with Schools Program, 2014, 1.

102 Keith Guthrie, "Santa Margarita Crossing," Handbook, accessed November 20, 2020. **https://www.tshaonline.org//handbook/entries/santa-margarita-crossing.**

103 Guthrie, "Santa Margarita Crossing."

104 Guthrie, "Santa Margarita Crossing."

105 Alicia A. Garza, "Casa Blanca, TX," Handbook, accessed December 09, 2020, https://**www.tshaonline.org/handbook/entries/casa-blanca-tx.**

106 J. Frank Dobie, Coronado's Children: Tales of Lost Mines and Buried Treasures of the Southwest, New York: Grosset & Dunlap, 1930, 96.

107 Dobie, Coronado's Children, 96.

108 Clotilde P. Garcia, "Garza Montemayor, Juan Jose de la," Handbook, accessed December 09, 2020, **https://tshaonline.org/handbook/entries/garza-montemayorjuan-jose-de-la**; See also, "Casa Blanca Land Grant Historical Marker," **http://www.stxmaps.com/go/texas-historical-marker-casa- blanca-land-grant.**

109 Garcia, "Garza Montemayor, Juan Jose de la."

110 Ibid.

111 Dobie, Coronado's Children, 95.

112 Ibid, 97.

113 Ibid, 97.

114 Keith Guthrie, "Fort Lipantitlan," Handbook, accessed December 09, 2020, **https:// www.tshaonline.org/handbook/entries/fort-lipantitlan.**

115 Rachel Bluntzer Hébert, The Lost Colony: San Patricio de Hibernia, Burnet, Texas: Eakin, 1981, 15.

116 Thonoff, "San Patricio Trail."

117 Dobie, Coronado's Children, 95.

118 Garcia, "Garza Montemayor, Juan Jose de la."

119 Corpus Christi Star, December 23, 1848, 2, col. 2 & 3.

120 Amelia W. Williams, "Kinney, Henry Lawrence," Handbook, accessed December 09, 2020, **https://www.tshaonline.org/handbook/entries/kinney-henry-lawrence.**

121 Fort Casa Blanca Historical Marker, JimWellsCounty,http:**www.fortwiki.com/ Fort_Casa_Blanca.**

122 Fort Casa Blanca Historical Marker.

123 Walter Foster, "Tribute to Deceased Pioneer Rancher [Wallis Dunn Wade]," obituary, [newspaper not recorded], Thursday, November 24, 1938.

124 A.M.French, Wm. Adams, J.C. Bluntzer, and J.H.Gallagher, Affidavits, Filed: Dec. 11, 1912, Recorded, Vol. "87" pp. 501-505, deed Records, Nueces County, Texas, Abstract of Title for A.H. Knolle, p. 177.

125 Garza, "Casa Blanca, TX."

126 Bill Walraven, "Wade Ranch auction will be end of an era," Corpus Christi CallerTimes, Wednesday, May 29, 1985, 2B.

127 Copy of Last Will and Testament of John Wade, Notice in Probate Dated June 13, 1898. Recorded: Vol. "H" p. 255-8 prob. Minutes N.C. No. 86 Estate of John Wade, deceased #625, 121- 123.

128 Garza, "Sandia, TX," Handbook, accessed November 19, 2020, **https://www.tshaonline.org/handbook/entries/sandia-tx.**
129 Garza, "Casa Blanca, TX."
130 Garza, "Casa Blanca, TX."

131 Warranty Deed, April 26, 1907; Filed June 11, 1907; Recorded July 9, 1907, Vol. 28, pp. 223-226, Nueces County Deed Records.

50 Years of Milking Jerseys

Knolle Jersey Farms 1928-1978

132 "Old Masterman is Dead: For 16 Years Had No Peer," Corpus Christi Caller, Sunday, February 1, 1948, 37.

133 J.F. Cavanaugh, "How do you raise 1,600 calves a year?", Jersey Journal, April 20, 1961, 25.

134 Grady Stiles, "World's Largest Jersey Farm," Hoard's Dairyman, November 10, 1951, 853; 873.

135 "The Knolle Brothers Know Their Jerseys," Humble Farm Family, August 1952, pp. 2-6. This is the most comprehensive article about Knolle Jersey Farms, providing an overall look at each area of the Farm, its employees, and the Knolle innovations of the time. The photographs provide detailed insights into each area of production.

136 J.F. Cavanaugh, "Feeding 5,500 Jerseys," Jersey Journal, [not known], 24.

137 Russ Oleson, "Man from Home of Breed Handles Show Jerseys for South Texas Ranch," San Antonio Express, Sunday, Oct. 26, 1952, 8.

138 J.F. Cavanaugh, "Two Century Sires are Backbone of Knolle Breeding Program," Jersey Journal, May 20, 1961, 62-63.

139 Sam Whitlow, "They Protect Livestock," The Texas Farmer-Stockman, October 1965, 8. The front page of this edition features a photograph of Ed Knolle and states, "Ed Knolle of Sandia is chairman of the Texas Animal

Health Commission, which has a vital role in maintaining health of Texas livestock and poultry, valued at $1,063,000,000."

140 Plaque presented to C.E. "Ed" Knolle by Texas Animal Health Commission. This plaque includes the exact dates of Ed's service as chairman and as member, Knolle Family Papers.

141 "Welcome to South Texas," Better Ranches & Farms, supplement to the Corpus Christi Caller, Wednesday, May 31, 1962, 2.

142 "1961 Master Breeder Award," Jersey Journal, June 20, 1961, pp. 23-24; See also "Master Breeder Award Certificate" presented to Ed Knolle by American Jersey Cattle Club, June 7, 1961, Knolle Family Papers.

143 "Knolle Jersey Farms—1967," Jersey Journal, June 5, 1967, pp. 39-41.

144 "Miss Louise Knolle of Sandia, daughter of Mr. and Mrs. Ed Knolle of the famed Knolle Jersey Farms in South Texas," cover page photograph, The Texas Farmer Stockman, November 1961.

145 "Knolle Jersey Farms—1967," Jersey Journal, June 5, 1967, 39-41.

146 Jersey Journal, cover page, November 20, 1965.

147 "Knolle Jersey Farms—1967," Jersey Journal, June 5, 1967, 39-41.

148 "Knolle Jersey Farms—1967," Jersey Journal, June 5, 1967, 39-41

149 "Charles Edward Knolle," obituary, Alice Echo News Journal, https://**www.alicetx.com/article/20100212/Obituaries/3021299 7 4.**

150 Plaque presented to The Knolle Family: Centennial Leaders by Texas A & M University, April 6, 1976, Knolle Family Papers.